MW00959815

AUSTRALIA TRAVEL GUIDE
2025

An Atlas Road Map to Sydney, The Great Barrier Reef, Uluru, Melbourne, Tasmania, Perth, Darwin, Gold Coast, Whitsundays, Kangaroo & Fraser Islands

By

ETHAN J. MCNALLY

WELCOME TO AUSTRALIA

(Outer Map of Australia)

COPYRIGHT

DISCLAIMER

The information provided in this eBook, **"AUSTRALIA TRAVEL GUIDE 2025,"** authored by **Ethan J. McNally**, is intended for general informational purposes only. Readers are advised to use the content as a guide.

Legal Compliance

The author and publisher have made efforts to comply with copyright and intellectual property laws. If any inadvertent infringement is identified, it is unintentional, and the author encourages notification for prompt correction.

Conclusion:

"AUSTRALIA TRAVEL GUIDE 2025," is a tool for inspiration and planning, but it does not substitute personalized travel advice or professional consultation. Readers should exercise prudence and diligence in their travel endeavors.

By using this guide, readers acknowledge and accept the terms of this disclaimer. The author and publisher disclaim any liability for outcomes resulting from the use or interpretation of the information provided herein. **Travel safely and enjoy the wonders of Australia with an informed and discerning mindset.**

About The Author

Ethan J. McNally is the person who authored "AUSTRALIA TRAVEL GUIDE 2025." **Ethan** loves exploring different cultures and places, and he wants to share his excitement and knowledge with you through this guide.

A Passionate Traveler:

Ethan started traveling to understand the unique stories of each place. He's been to bustling cities and Nations, remote landscapes, and hidden spots, all to discover what makes each destination special.

His Love for Australia:

Ethan's love for **Australia** runs deep. Through multiple visits, he has immersed himself in the region's vibrant neighborhoods and pedaled along its scenic canals. **His encounters shape the authentic insights that make this guide an indispensable companion.**

Master of Insider Tips:

Ethan is good at finding hidden gems and authentic experiences. **He wants to share these with you so you can have a memorable trip beyond the usual tourist spots.**

Author's Vision:

Ethan's vision with this guide is to help you explore Australia like a pro. Exploring **Australia** like a pro means to dive into **its culture, history, and vibrant atmosphere,** even without experiencing confusion in the long run or being worried about anything.

Let **Ethan** be your reliable companion, unveiling the mysteries of **Australia** and ensuring your journey transcends mere travel, transforming into **a truly enriching experience.**

Table of Contents

- **The Great Barrier Reef**: Best spots for snorkeling, diving, and reef tours
- **Cairns and Port Douglas**: Gateway cities to the reef and Daintree Rainforest
- **Gold Coast**: Theme parks, beaches, and nightlife
- **Brisbane**: River city attractions, South Bank, and local arts scene
- **Whitsunday Islands**: Whitehaven Beach, sailing adventures, and island hopping

CHAPTER FOUR: Uluru, Outback, and Northern Territory Adventures

- **Uluru (Ayers Rock):** Aboriginal culture, sunset views, and the Field of Light art installation
- **Alice Springs**: Desert landscapes, cultural sites, and camel tours
- **Kakadu National Park**: Wildlife, waterfalls, and ancient rock art
- **Darwin**: Mindil Beach markets, WWII history, and crocodile encounters
- **Exploring the Outback**: Unique road trips, safety tips, and iconic stops

CHAPTER FIVE: Melbourne, Tasmania, and Victoria's Coastline

- **Melbourne**: Arts, culture, dining, and famous laneways
- **The Great Ocean Road**: Scenic coastal drives, Twelve Apostles, and surf spots
- **Phillip Island**: Penguin Parade, wildlife encounters, and local beaches
- **Tasmania**: Hobart, Cradle Mountain, Freycinet National Park, and local food

CHAPTER SIX: Perth, Western Australia, and South Australian Wonders

- **Perth**: Swan River, beaches, Kings Park, and urban attractions
- **Margaret River**: Wine, gourmet food, and surf culture
- **Ningaloo Reef**: Whale shark experiences and pristine reefs
- **Adelaide and Surrounds**: Barossa Valley wineries, festivals, and coastal spots
- **Kangaroo Island**: Wildlife, coastal scenery, and secluded beaches

CHAPTER SEVEN: Seven-Day Itinerary for Australia's Highlights

- Day 1: Sydney
- Day 2: Blue Mountains
- Day 3: Cairns and Great Barrier Reef

- Day 4: Whitsunday Islands
- Day 5: Uluru
- Day 6: Melbourne
- Day 7: Great Ocean Road

OTHER BOOKS RECOMMENDATION

A KIND GESTURE

Chapter One:
Introduction to Australia

Overview of Australia

Australia is a vast and fascinating country, stretching over 7.7 million square kilometers. **It's the world's sixth-largest country and unique in many ways.**

Surrounded by the Indian and Pacific Oceans, Australia is both a country and a continent, known for its remarkable range of landscapes, from red deserts to lush rainforests, sunny beaches, and snowy mountains.

• **Geography**

Australia lies in the Southern Hemisphere, so its seasons are opposite those in the Northern Hemisphere.

For example, summer in Australia falls from December to February, while winter occurs from June to August. This makes it a popular travel destination, especially during the Northern Hemisphere's winter.

Australia has six states and two main territories, each with unique landscapes and features.

For example:

- New South Wales (NSW)

Home to Sydney, the country's largest city, and the Blue Mountains, known for their rugged cliffs and eucalyptus forests.

- Queensland

Famous for the Great Barrier Reef, one of the world's largest coral reefs, as well as tropical rainforests and sunny beaches along the Gold Coast.

- Victoria

Known for its vibrant capital, Melbourne, and the scenic Great Ocean Road, where visitors can see coastal cliffs and rock formations like the Twelve Apostles.

- Western Australia

The largest state, featuring Perth, the Pinnacles Desert, and Ningaloo Reef, where you can swim alongside whale sharks.

- South Australia

Known for the Barossa Valley, a popular wine region, and Kangaroo Island, where you can find sea lions, koalas, and, of course, kangaroos.

- Tasmania

An island state with rainforests, mountains, and stunning national parks like Cradle Mountain-Lake St Clair.

Australia is often divided into four main geographical areas: the Eastern Highlands, the Central Lowlands, the Western Plateau, and the coastal areas.

1. Eastern Highlands

Also known as the Great Dividing Range, this is Australia's largest mountain range, stretching from Queensland down through New South Wales to Victoria. This area includes famous mountains like Mount Kosciuszko, the tallest peak on the mainland, and supports a range of forests and highland plants.

2. Central Lowlands

This vast, flat region stretches across the center of the country, covering parts of Queensland, New South Wales, and South Australia. **Here, you'll find some of Australia's most iconic features, like Lake Eyre, the largest lake in Australia, which only fills with water during rare, heavy rains.** The Outback also lies here, known for its dry, remote deserts and towns.

3. Western Plateau

Covering most of Western Australia, the Northern Territory, and parts of South Australia, this area is a large desert region with rocky plains and ancient rock formations. **Famous natural landmarks here include Uluru (Ayers Rock) and Kata Tjuta (the Olgas), which are sacred** to Aboriginal people and display stunning colors at sunrise and sunset.

4. Coastal Areas

Australia is famous for its long coastline, stretching for about 35,000 kilometers. **This includes some of the world's best beaches, like Bondi Beach in Sydney, Whitehaven Beach in Queensland, and Cable Beach in Western Australia.** Australia's coasts are ideal for surfing, swimming, snorkeling, and other water sports.

• Climate

Because Australia is so large, its climate varies widely from region to region. It has several climate zones, including tropical, desert, Mediterranean, and temperate.

- Tropical Climate

Northern Australia, including parts of Queensland, Northern Territory, and Western Australia, has a tropical climate with hot, humid summers and warm, dry winters. This area includes the Great Barrier Reef and the Daintree Rainforest. Cities like **Darwin and Cairns experience wet and dry seasons rather than the four traditional seasons,** with heavy rains during the wet season from November to April.

- Desert Climate

Central Australia, also known as the Outback, has a desert climate with very hot summers and cooler winters. This area gets little rainfall, and temperatures can soar over 40°C (104°F) in summer. **Places like Alice Springs and Uluru lie in this desert region.**

- Mediterranean Climate

Southern Australia, especially around Perth and Adelaide, enjoys a Mediterranean climate with warm, dry summers and mild, wet winters. This climate is great for vineyards, making it perfect for the famous wine regions like the Barossa Valley in South Australia.

- Temperate Climate

The southeastern part of Australia, including Sydney, Melbourne, and Tasmania, has a temperate climate. Here, summers are warm, and winters are mild. In the highlands of New South Wales and Victoria, like in the Snowy Mountains, you can even experience snow in winter, which attracts skiers.

• Diverse Landscapes

Australia's landscapes are incredibly diverse, each with its own unique plants, animals, and natural beauty. Some highlights include:

- Rainforests

Northern Queensland is home to some of the world's oldest rainforests, like **the Daintree Rainforest.** This area is rich in biodiversity and has plants and animals found nowhere else on Earth, including tree kangaroos and the endangered cassowary bird.

- Deserts

Australia is one of the driest continents, with famous deserts like **the Simpson Desert and the Great Victoria Desert.** These deserts are home to unique wildlife, such as dingoes, desert lizards, and spinifex grass.

- Reefs

The Great Barrier Reef, stretching over 2,300 kilometers, is one of Australia's most famous natural attractions. It's the world's largest coral reef system and is home to diverse marine life, including colorful fish, turtles, and coral species. **Ningaloo Reef in Western Australia also offers incredible underwater experiences.**

- Mountain Ranges

The Australian Alps in the southeast offer cool mountain climates and attract visitors who enjoy hiking in the summer and skiing in the winter. Mount Kosciuszko, Australia's tallest mountain, is part of this range.

- Beaches and Coastlines

Australia is world-renowned for its beautiful beaches, where visitors can enjoy activities like swimming, surfing, and relaxing on the shore.

Whitehaven Beach in the Whitsundays is famous for its pure white sand, and Bondi Beach in Sydney is iconic for surfers and beachgoers alike.

Why Visit in 2025?

Australia is an exciting place to visit in 2025, with many special events, festivals, and travel trends that make it a great choice for travelers.

From world-famous festivals to exciting sports events and nature adventures, Australia has something for everyone.

Here are some key reasons why visiting Australia in 2025 is an excellent idea.

1. Exciting Festivals and Celebrations

Australia is known for its lively festivals, celebrating everything from music and film to food and culture. Here are some of the biggest and most popular festivals happening in 2025:

- Sydney Festival (January)

The Sydney Festival kicks off the new year with performances, art installations, and fun activities across the city. Expect open-air concerts, dance performances, and art displays in places like Hyde Park and Darling Harbour. This festival has something for everyone, whether you love music, theater, or just exploring Sydney's creative side.

- Australian Open (January)

Sports fans should not miss the Australian Open tennis tournament in Melbourne. As one of the four major tennis tournaments in the world, it attracts top players and thousands of fans. Watching a live match at Melbourne Park is thrilling, and the event also has food stalls, kids' activities, and music to keep everyone entertained.

- Adelaide Fringe (February-March)

Known as the largest arts festival in the Southern Hemisphere, Adelaide Fringe has over 1,000 performances, including comedy, music, dance, and more. You'll find fun shows at theatres, parks, and even on the streets of Adelaide. With its fun atmosphere, this festival is great for both locals and visitors.

- Vivid Sydney (May-June)

This incredible light and music festival lights up Sydney's landmarks like the Opera House, Harbour Bridge, and Circular Quay with colorful displays.

The event also features concerts and talks by artists and musicians. Vivid Sydney is popular among tourists and locals alike, bringing the city to life in a way that's fun for all ages.

- Melbourne International Comedy Festival (March-April)

Melbourne's famous comedy festival brings comedians from all over the world for a month of laughter and good times. Shows range from big performances by famous comedians to small, funny acts in cozy venues. Whether you're a fan of stand-up, improv, or sketch comedy, this festival is sure to deliver laughs.

- Splendour in the Grass (July)

This is one of Australia's biggest music festivals, held in Byron Bay. Featuring popular artists from Australia and around the world, this three-day festival draws thousands of music fans. It's set in a beautiful area with food stalls, art installations, and camping options for those who want to stay overnight.

2. Major Sports Events and Competitions

Australia is home to major sports events that attract fans from around the globe. In 2025, several big events make it an especially exciting time to visit.

- The Ashes (Cricket)

Every few years, Australia and England compete in The Ashes, one of the oldest cricket rivalries in the world.

The Ashes series in 2025 will include test matches across Australia, drawing huge crowds in cities like Sydney, Melbourne, and Brisbane. It's a great chance to experience cricket culture in Australia.

- Formula 1 Australian Grand Prix (April)

Held in Melbourne's Albert Park, the Australian Grand Prix is an exciting event for car racing fans.

Visitors can watch the world's top drivers race around the track and enjoy other events, including car displays, food stalls, and live music.

- Australian Football League (AFL) Finals (September)

Aussie rules football is one of Australia's most popular sports, and the AFL Finals in September bring together fans from all over.

The Grand Final in Melbourne is a thrilling experience, with tens of thousands of fans cheering for their favorite teams at the Melbourne Cricket Ground (MCG).

- Sydney to Hobart Yacht Race (December)

This annual sailing race starts in Sydney on Boxing Day (December 26) and ends in Hobart, Tasmania.

Watching the yachts sail out of Sydney Harbour is a festive tradition, and seeing them arrive in Hobart is a celebration with plenty of food and entertainment.

3. Unique Travel Trends in 2025

Travel trends in Australia for 2025 show a strong interest in nature, culture, and sustainability.

Travelers are looking for new ways to explore and experience the country responsibly.

- Eco-Tourism

With Australia's focus on protecting its natural areas, eco-tourism is growing.

Places like **Daintree Rainforest in Queensland and Kakadu National Park** in the Northern Territory are popular spots where visitors can see Australia's unique wildlife while supporting conservation efforts.

Many tours and accommodations are now eco-friendly, helping to protect Australia's natural beauty.

- Aboriginal Cultural Experiences

Visitors are increasingly interested in learning about Australia's rich Aboriginal heritage. In places like **Uluru** and **Kakadu National Park**, travelers can join cultural tours led by Indigenous guides, who share traditional stories, bushcraft skills, and local art.

These experiences give visitors a chance to understand Australia's oldest culture in a respectful way.

- Food and Wine Tourism

Australia has excellent food and wine, and places like the **Barossa Valley** in South Australia and **Yarra Valley** in Victoria are top destinations for food lovers.

In 2025, food and wine tours are expected to be popular, especially those offering hands-on experiences like cooking classes, wine tastings, and farm visits.

- Road Trips and Remote Travel

With Australia's large, open spaces and good road networks, road trips are a popular way to explore the country.

Scenic routes like the **Great Ocean Road** in Victoria and the **Savannah Way** through Northern Australia allow travelers to see coastal views, rainforests, and the Outback.

Many visitors are also exploring remote destinations like Ningaloo Reef and The Kimberley, which offer breathtaking scenery and fewer crowds.

4. Spectacular Natural Events

Australia is known for its amazing natural wonders, and some special events in 2025 make it an ideal time to visit for nature lovers.

- Coral Spawning at the Great Barrier Reef (November)

Each year, the coral in the Great Barrier Reef spawns in a beautiful display, releasing millions of tiny coral eggs and sperm into the water.

This usually happens in November, and it's an unforgettable sight for divers and snorkelers. The reef comes alive with colors and sea life during this period.

- Wildflower Season in Western Australia (August-October)

Western Australia has one of the largest wildflower seasons in the world, with over 12,000 species blooming across the state.

From August to October, fields in places like Kalbarri National Park and Kings Park in Perth are filled with colorful wildflowers, making it a perfect time for nature walks and photography.

- Whale Watching (May-November)

Whale watching is a popular activity along Australia's coast from May to November. **Spots like Hervey Bay in Queensland and Albany in Western Australia are excellent for seeing humpback whales up close as they migrate along the coast.**

5. New Attractions and Experiences

2025 also brings some new attractions and experiences for visitors. Many cities and popular areas are upgrading their facilities, making it easier and more enjoyable for travelers.

- Sydney Modern Project

The Art Gallery of New South Wales recently expanded with new galleries and outdoor spaces, making it an exciting destination for art lovers. The Sydney Modern Project includes indigenous art, contemporary art, and immersive exhibitions that highlight Australia's creative talent.

- Indigenous Art Trails

New art trails are being established in areas like Alice Springs and the Northern Territory, where visitors can follow paths showcasing indigenous rock art and sculptures. These trails give visitors a way to connect with Aboriginal culture while enjoying Australia's natural landscapes.

- Renewed Walking Trails

Australia's famous walking trails, like the Overland Track in Tasmania and the Larapinta Trail in the Northern Territory, have been upgraded for safety and accessibility. These trails offer hikers incredible views of mountains, deserts, and forests.

Planning Your Trip

Planning a trip to Australia can be exciting, and a little preparation can help you enjoy the adventure without any hassle.

Here's a simple guide on what you need to know about visas, health and safety tips, travel essentials, and other important information to make your Australian trip enjoyable and stress-free.

1. Visas and Entry Requirements

Before heading to Australia, all visitors need to arrange a visa. Most tourists can get a visa online, making it quick and easy. Here are the main types:

- Electronic Travel Authority (ETA)

This is a popular choice for people from countries like the United States, Canada, Japan, and Singapore. An ETA lets you stay in Australia for up to three months and is easy to apply for online. Just visit the official Australian government website, and you'll have your visa within minutes.

- eVisitor Visa

This visa is similar to the ETA and is available for travelers from the European Union. The eVisitor visa also allows for stays of up to three months and can be applied for online without any application fee.

- Visitor Visa (Subclass 600)

For those wanting to stay longer than three months, a Visitor Visa can allow stays of up to 12 months. If you're planning a longer trip or visiting family, this is a good option. You'll need to submit some documents, like proof of funds or an invitation letter from family or friends in Australia.

It's a good idea to apply for your visa a few weeks before your trip, just in case there are any delays. And remember to bring a printed copy of your visa approval along with your passport.

2. When to Go

Australia has four seasons, but they happen at opposite times of the year compared to the Northern Hemisphere. The breakdown below will show you what each season has to offer:

- Summer (December-February)

Summer in Australia is great for beach trips and outdoor activities. **Places like Sydney and Gold Coast come alive with sunbathers and surfers.** However, it can get very hot, especially in the Outback regions near **Uluru and Alice Springs.**

- Autumn (March-May)

Autumn has milder temperatures and is a great time to visit popular cities **like Melbourne and Sydney.** This season is also perfect for exploring vineyards in places like the **Barossa Valley** in South Australia.

- Winter (June-August)

Winter in Australia can be mild in most areas, but the southern regions, like **Tasmania and Victoria,** can get chilly. However, winter is perfect for visiting the tropical regions like **Cairns and the Great Barrier Reef,** where the weather stays warm and pleasant.

- Spring (September-November)

Spring brings warm temperatures and blooming flowers. It's a beautiful time to visit **Perth** or explore the national parks, like **Kings Park and Rottnest Island,** which are filled with colorful wildflowers.

3. Health Tips and Vaccinations

Australia has high health and safety standards, so you won't need many vaccinations to visit. However, here are a few health tips to keep in mind:

- Recommended Vaccinations

Ensure you're not missing out on your routine vaccinations, like rubella, measles or mumps. If you're coming from a country with a high risk of yellow fever, you may need to show proof of vaccination upon arrival.

- Sun Protection

Australia has one of the highest rates of UV radiation, so sun safety is very important. Always wear sunscreen, sunglasses, and a hat when spending time outdoors. Many visitors are surprised at how strong the sun can be, even on cloudy days. The Australian government has a simple rule called "Slip, Slop, Slap" – slip on a shirt, slop on sunscreen, and slap on a hat.

- Mosquito Protection

If you're visiting tropical areas, like the **Daintree Rainforest or Kakadu National Park,** use insect repellent to avoid mosquito bites, which can sometimes carry diseases like dengue fever.

- Stay Hydrated

Australia's warm climate means you can get dehydrated easily, especially in places like the Outback. So, ensure you always stay hydrated.

4. Safety Tips and Emergency Information

Australia is a very safe country for travelers, but it's still smart to follow basic safety guidelines to ensure a smooth trip.

- Emergency Numbers

The emergency phone number in Australia is 000. You can call this number for police, fire, or medical emergencies. Make a note of this number, especially if you're planning to explore more remote areas.

- Beach Safety

In Australia, there are possibilities for strong current in beaches, even though they are beautiful places. **Always swim between the red and yellow flags on patrolled beaches like Bondi Beach or Surfers Paradise.** Lifeguards are there to keep swimmers safe, so make sure to follow any warnings or signs.

- Wildlife Awareness

Australia has unique wildlife, some of which can be dangerous. If you're hiking in the bush or exploring areas with wildlife, keep an eye out for snakes and spiders. It's best to avoid touching animals you don't recognize.

If you're planning a trip to the northern parts of Australia, such as Darwin or Cairns, be mindful of saltwater crocodiles in rivers and estuaries.

- Driving in Australia

Australians drive on the left side of the road, so if you're renting a car, take some time to adjust.

Many people enjoy driving along scenic routes like the Great Ocean Road.

Remember to fill up on gas and have a map or GPS, as some rural areas have few gas stations and poor cell service.

5. Money Matters and Budgeting

Australia is a developed country with a strong economy, so costs can add up, especially in major cities like **Sydney and Melbourne.**

Here are a few tips to manage your budget:

- Currency

Australia uses the Australian Dollar (AUD), which you can get at currency exchange centers or ATMs at the airport.

Credit and debit cards are widely accepted in most places, but it's helpful to carry a small amount of cash for remote areas or small shops.

- Budget Tips

Food and accommodation can be expensive in city centers.

To save money, consider staying in hostels or budget hotels, and look for affordable meals at food courts or local markets. **Places like Queen Victoria Market in Melbourne offer delicious food at reasonable prices.**

- Tipping

Tipping is not expected in Australia, as service charges are usually included in bills. If you receive exceptional service, you can tip, but it's not required.

6. Packing Essentials

Australia's climate can vary, so pack clothing based on the season and the regions you plan to visit.

- Light Clothing for Summer

For warm regions like Queensland, pack lightweight clothes, swimwear, and a good pair of sandals or water shoes if you plan to visit beaches or waterfalls.

- Warm Layers for Winter

In southern areas like Tasmania or Melbourne, winter can be chilly, so bring warm layers and a waterproof jacket, especially if you're visiting during the cooler months.

- Comfortable Shoes

This should be a MUST for you to bring along since there are so much to see and do in Australia.

Whether you're walking through city streets, hiking in national parks, or exploring beaches, a good pair of shoes will keep your feet happy.

- Adapters for Electronics

Australia uses a Type I plug, so if you're coming from a country with a different plug type, bring an adapter. Many hotels offer adapters, but having your own is convenient.

7. Staying Connected

Australia has reliable Wi-Fi in most cities and towns, with many cafes, hotels, and public spaces offering free Wi-Fi. **However, if you're planning to travel to remote areas, like The Kimberley or Fraser Island, keep in mind that internet access may be limited. Here are some tips**:

- SIM Cards

If you're planning a longer stay, consider purchasing a local SIM card from companies like Telstra or Optus.

These companies have good coverage across most of Australia, and a prepaid plan will allow you to make calls, use data, and send texts affordably.

- Emergency Contacts

Make sure to share your travel plans with friends or family back home, especially if you're visiting remote areas. Having someone aware of your travel plans is helpful in case of emergencies.

Best Times to Visit

Australia is a big country with seasons opposite to those in the Northern Hemisphere.

When it's winter in places like the United States or Europe, it's summer in Australia. Because of its size, Australia's weather changes a lot from place to place, so the best time to visit depends on where you're going and what you'd like to do.

Whether you're planning to see the Great Barrier Reef, visit Sydney's beaches, or experience the Outback, here's a simple guide to the seasons and what each one offers.

• **Understanding Australia's Seasons**

Since Australia is in the Southern Hemisphere, its seasons are flipped compared to those in the Northern Hemisphere:

- **Summer:** December to February

- **Autumn:** March to May

- **Winter**: June to August

- **Spring:** September to November

Each season brings its own weather, with unique highlights and events. Let's look at what makes each season special and which destinations shine during these times.

• **Summer (December to February)**

- Weather and Temperatures

Summer in Australia is generally warm to hot. Coastal areas like **Sydney, Melbourne, and Brisbane** have warm temperatures, usually around 25°C to 30°C (77°F to 86°F). In the Outback, near **Alice Springs and Uluru,** temperatures can rise much higher, sometimes above 40°C (104°F). The northern parts of Australia, like **Darwin and Cairns,** experience wet season rains with high humidity and frequent storms.

• **Best Places to Visit**

- Sydney

Summer is a fantastic time to visit Sydney. The weather is warm, and the beaches, like **Bondi and Manly,** are popular for swimming and surfing.

Sydney also hosts exciting events like the famous **New Year's Eve fireworks** at

Sydney Harbour, drawing crowds from around the world.

- Melbourne

Known for its mix of beaches and cultural festivals, Melbourne is bustling in the summer. It's also the time for the **Australian Open,** one of the four Grand Slam tennis tournaments, which draws many visitors.

- Great Barrier Reef

This is a popular time to visit the Great Barrier Reef off the coast of **Cairns.** The waters are warm, and although it's the wet season in the northern tropics, it's still a good time for snorkeling and diving. Be mindful of stinger season, when jellyfish are common, and wear protective suits for safety.

• Events

Summer brings lively events, such as **Australia Day** on January 26, with celebrations, parades, and fireworks across the country.

• **Autumn (March to May)**

- **Weather and Temperatures**

Autumn in Australia offers milder weather, with temperatures ranging from 15°C to 25°C (59°F to 77°F) in the southern parts. The Outback remains warm but more comfortable than in summer, while the northern areas start to cool and dry out as the wet season ends.

• **Best Places to Visit**

- **Tasmania**

Autumn is ideal for exploring Tasmania's beautiful wilderness areas, like **Cradle Mountain and Freycinet National Park.** The weather is mild, and the autumn colors create stunning landscapes.

- Adelaide and Barossa Valley

For wine lovers, this is grape harvest season in regions like **Barossa Valley** near Adelaide. You can enjoy wine tours and tastings and see the vineyards during a peaceful and scenic time of year.

- Canberra

The nation's capital is known for its colorful displays of autumn leaves. The **Canberra Balloon Spectacular** also takes place during this season, filling the skies with bright hot air balloons.

• Events

Autumn brings festivals like **Vivid Sydney,** a festival of lights, music, and ideas, which usually takes place in May. Vivid transforms Sydney's landmarks, such as the Opera House, with vibrant light displays.

- **Winter (June to August)**

- **Weather and Temperatures**

Winter in Australia is different from winter in colder countries. In places like **Sydney and Brisbane**, temperatures stay mild, around 10°C to 20°C (50°F to 68°F).

However, southern cities like **Melbourne and Hobart** can get chilly, and some areas even get snow, such as the **Australian Alps.**

Meanwhile, the northern regions, including **Darwin and the Great Barrier Reef,** enjoy warm, dry weather, making winter a popular time for tropical destinations.

- **Best Places to Visit**

- **Northern Australia**

Winter is the perfect season to visit tropical northern areas.

In **Darwin and Kakadu National Park,** the weather is dry and pleasant, making it ideal for hiking and wildlife watching.

Cairns and the Great Barrier Reef also experience sunny, calm weather, making water activities enjoyable.

- Australian Alps

Winter is the ski season in Australia's snowy regions, like **Perisher and Thredbo** in New South Wales and **Mount Buller** in Victoria.

It's a great time to enjoy skiing, snowboarding, and cozy lodges.

- The Outback

Winter is the best time to explore Outback areas like **Uluru and Alice Springs.** With cooler temperatures, it's easier to hike, camp, and see famous sites like Uluru and Kings Canyon without the intense heat.

• **Events**

Winter sees festivals like **Darwin Festival** in August, celebrating local arts and culture, and **Dark Mofo** in Tasmania, which combines art, food, and music in unique ways.

• **Spring (September to November)**

- **Weather and Temperatures**

Spring is a pleasant season, with temperatures warming up across the country. Southern areas, like **Sydney and Melbourne,** experience temperatures from 15°C to 25°C (59°F to 77°F).

In the north, it's warmer and drier, while the Outback also enjoys comfortable conditions.

- **Best Places to Visit**

- Whitsunday Islands

Spring is perfect for a visit to the Whitsundays, known for their crystal-clear waters and white sand beaches.

The Great Barrier Reef is also stunning during this time, with comfortable temperatures and excellent visibility for diving and snorkeling.

- Perth and Western Australia

Spring brings a burst of wildflowers in Western Australia.

Kings Park in Perth becomes a carpet of color with native wildflowers blooming. It's also a good time to explore the coastal areas, like **Rottnest Island,** where you can spot quokkas and enjoy the beaches.

- Blue Mountains

Located near Sydney, the Blue Mountains are beautiful in spring.

The warmer weather makes it easy to explore trails, scenic lookouts, and waterfalls like **Wentworth Falls.**

The region's famous **Three Sisters** rock formation is a must-see.

• **Events**

Spring is festival season across Australia. **Melbourne Cup Day,** "the race that stops a nation," takes place in November, drawing huge crowds. In Canberra, the **Floriade Festival** celebrates spring with thousands of blooming flowers.

• **Quick Summary of Australia's Best Seasons by Region**

- **Northern Australia (Darwin, Great Barrier Reef)**

Best visited during the dry winter months (June-August) when the weather is warm and sunny.

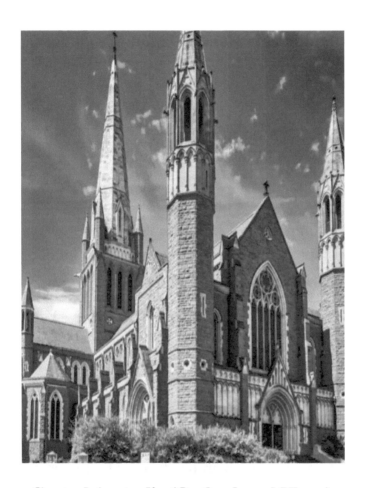

- Central Australia (Outback and Uluru)

Comfortable to visit in autumn or winter (March-August) to avoid the intense summer heat.

- Southern Australia (Sydney, Melbourne, Adelaide)

Ideal for visits in spring or autumn (September-November or March-May), with mild, comfortable temperatures.

- Tasmania

Autumn brings beautiful scenery with fall colors, while summer is great for outdoor activities.

• Choosing the Best Time for Your Activities

- Beach and Water Sports

For a beach vacation in places like the Gold Coast, Sydney, or the Whitsunday Islands, summer (which runs from December to February) is the most popular season, but spring (September to November) is also a great time with pleasant temperatures and fewer crowds.

- Hiking and Nature Walks

Spring and autumn are ideal for hiking in areas like the Blue Mountains or national parks near Perth, as temperatures are mild, and nature is full of life.

- Outback and Wildlife

Winter is best for seeing the Outback, where you can explore without the extreme heat. Winter and spring are also great for wildlife, as animals are more active in cooler weather.

Chapter Two: Sydney and New South Wales Highlights

Sydney

Sydney is one of Australia's most famous cities. With its mix of stunning architecture, world-famous beaches, and beautiful waterfront areas, Sydney offers plenty of things to see and do.

From the iconic Sydney Opera House and Harbour Bridge to the fun atmosphere at Bondi Beach and Darling Harbour, each spot has its own unique charm.

• Sydney Opera House

This is one of the most famous and recognizable buildings we have in the world today. It sits right on Sydney Harbour, with its unique white sails looking like they're floating on the water.

Danish architect **Jørn Utzon** designed the building, which opened in 1973. Today, the Opera House is known for its concerts, plays, and performances, as well as its impressive architecture.

Visitors can take a guided tour to learn more about the Opera House's design and history. You can walk around inside, see its concert halls, and even attend a show if there's one happening during your visit.

At night, the Opera House lights up, and sometimes special events, like **Vivid Sydney**, fill its sails with colorful lights, creating a fantastic view over the harbour.

• **Sydney Harbour Bridge**

The Sydney Harbour Bridge, often called "The Coathanger" because of its shape, connects the city's north and south shores.

Opened in 1932, it's made of steel and is one of the longest steel-arch bridges in the world. Walking across the bridge is a fun way to get amazing views of the city and the Opera House.

There's a dedicated pedestrian walkway, so you can stroll along at your own pace while looking out over the water and the city skyline.

For the adventurous, there's the **BridgeClimb** experience, which allows you to climb up to the top of the Harbour Bridge. This climb is led by a guide, who takes groups to the summit, 134 meters above the water.

At the top, climbers get a 360-degree view of Sydney, including sights like **Luna Park** and the **Royal Botanic Garden**.

The BridgeClimb is popular with visitors of all ages, and while it's safe and secure, it does take about three hours to complete, making it a memorable way to experience the bridge up close.

• **Bondi Beach**

Bondi Beach is Sydney's most famous beach, known for its golden sand, clear blue waters, and lively vibe. It's a perfect spot for swimming, sunbathing, and surfing. Bondi is especially popular in summer, when locals and tourists fill the beach to relax and enjoy the warm weather.

The waves at Bondi Beach attract surfers from all over, and even beginners can try their hand at surfing by taking lessons from local surf schools. If surfing isn't your thing, you can simply enjoy walking along the shoreline or trying out the **Bondi to Coogee coastal walk**. This scenic walk stretches for about six kilometers, passing other beautiful beaches like **Tamarama and Bronte Beach.** The views along the way are stunning, with cliffs, rock pools, and ocean views.

Bondi Beach is also known for its **Bondi Icebergs Pool**, a large oceanfront pool that's open year-round. Swimming at Icebergs Pool is a unique experience because it's right next to the ocean, and waves sometimes splash into the pool, blending the fresh and saltwater. Near Bondi, there are plenty of cafes, shops, and places to eat, offering a mix of Australian and international food.

• **Darling Harbour**

Darling Harbour is a lively waterfront area with entertainment, restaurants, and activities for all ages. It's located close to the city center, making it easy to get to by foot, ferry, or train. Darling Harbour has several attractions worth visiting, and you can easily spend a day exploring the area.

One of the main attractions is the **SEA LIFE Sydney Aquarium**, which showcases Australia's rich marine life, including sharks, rays, and a special exhibit on the Great Barrier Reef. The aquarium even has a "Shark Walk" where visitors can walk through a tunnel surrounded by sharks and other ocean animals. Kids and families often enjoy this experience, as it lets them get up close to the ocean's most famous creatures.

Another popular spot at Darling Harbour is the **Australian National Maritime Museum.**

• The map above shows distance (with time covered) from Sydney central to Australian National Maritime Museum

Here, visitors can learn about Australia's maritime history and see real ships, such as **HMAS Vampire**, a retired navy destroyer, and **James Craig,** a tall ship from the 19th century.

The museum also has interactive exhibits that teach about Australia's role in global sea trade and exploration.

For those looking to relax, the **Chinese Garden of Friendship** offers a quiet space with ponds, waterfalls, and traditional Chinese architecture.

Built as a gift from Sydney's sister city, Guangzhou, this garden is a peaceful place to sit and enjoy nature.

Darling Harbour is also known for its variety of restaurants and cafes along the waterfront. There are places that serve seafood, Asian cuisine, and Australian dishes, so visitors have plenty of options for lunch or dinner.

In the evenings, Darling Harbour comes alive with lights and sometimes hosts special events, like fireworks displays on weekends.

• **Why Sydney's Highlights Are Special**

Sydney is a city where modern city life meets natural beauty. With the Opera House, Harbour Bridge, Bondi Beach, and Darling Harbour, there's something for everyone, from architecture and history to outdoor fun and marine life.

- Cultural Icons

The Opera House and Harbour Bridge are symbols of Sydney and are well-loved by Australians and visitors alike. They offer both unique looks and rich histories.

- Beach Fun

Bondi Beach is a great place for both relaxation and adventure, where you can try surfing or just enjoy the sand and sun.

- Family-Friendly Entertainment

Darling Harbour is packed with things to do, from seeing sea creatures to enjoying a peaceful garden walk.

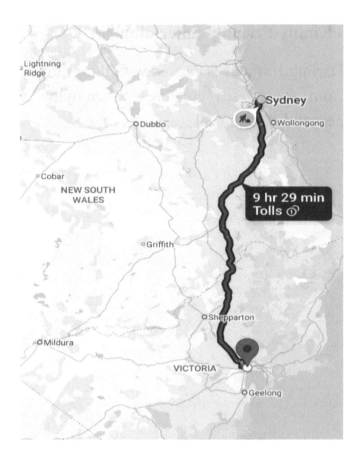

- **The map above shows distance (with time covered) from Melbourne to Sydney**

Blue Mountains

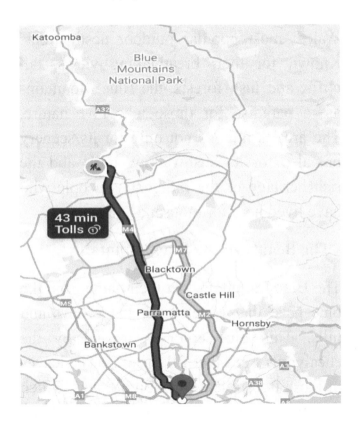

• The map above shows distance (with time covered) from Sydney central to the Blue Mountains

The Blue Mountains, located just a short drive west of Sydney, are one of New South Wales' most popular outdoor destinations. Known for their breathtaking views, tall cliffs, and lush forests, the Blue Mountains are a paradise for those who love nature. The area is famous not only for its scenery but also for its bushwalking trails and the rich heritage of the Indigenous people who have lived here for thousands of years.

• **The Beauty of the Blue Mountains**

The Blue Mountains get their name from the blue haze that hovers over the valleys and hills. This blue color is caused by the eucalyptus trees that fill the area. The leaves of these trees release fine oil droplets, which scatter sunlight and create the blue effect. It's a unique sight that adds a special touch to the landscape, making the mountains look almost magical, especially at sunrise and sunset.

The region has several must-see viewpoints that offer panoramic views of the valleys, cliffs, and forests below. One of the most famous is **Echo Point,** which provides an incredible view of the Three Sisters rock formation. These three tall sandstone peaks are one of Australia's most recognized natural landmarks.

• **Echo Point and the Three Sisters**

The Three Sisters is one of the main attractions in the Blue Mountains, drawing thousands of visitors every year. The Three Sisters are located near the town of **Katoomba** and are easily viewed from Echo Point. According to an old Indigenous legend, the three rocks represent three sisters who were turned to stone by a tribal elder to protect them. It's a story that reflects the connection Indigenous people have with the land and adds a layer of mystery to the landscape.

From Echo Point, you can take in the impressive views of the Three Sisters and the vast valley beyond. The site is perfect for photos, and there are often telescopes set up for those who want a closer look.

Visitors can also walk down into the valley through the **Giant Stairway,** which leads to the base of the Three Sisters.

This steep path has over 800 steps, so it's a bit of a workout, but it's worth the effort for those who want to see the rock formations up close.

• Bushwalking and Scenic World

Bushwalking, or hiking, is one of the most popular activities in the Blue Mountains.

There are numerous trails suited for different levels, from easy walks to more challenging hikes. Some trails lead through lush forests, while others offer spectacular views of cliffs and waterfalls.

For beginners, the **Prince Henry Cliff Walk** is a good choice. This trail stretches from **Leura to Katoomba** and follows the cliff tops, providing stunning views of the valley below.

It's a relatively easy walk, making it great for families and those new to bushwalking.

For those who want a unique experience without too much hiking, **Scenic World** is a fantastic option. Located in Katoomba, Scenic World offers attractions that showcase the Blue Mountains from different angles.

Here, you can take the **Scenic Railway**, which is one of the steepest railways in the world.

This thrilling ride descends into the Jamison Valley, giving passengers a chance to experience the beauty of the forest and cliffs up close.

Scenic World also has the Scenic Skyway, a cable car that glides across the valley, offering 360-degree views of the surrounding landscape. The cable car even has a glass floor, so you can see the forest directly below.

For those who prefer to stay grounded, the **Scenic Walkway** offers a peaceful stroll through the rainforest at the bottom of the valley.

• **Waterfalls and Natural Attractions**

The Blue Mountains are home to several beautiful waterfalls, which are perfect spots for a peaceful break during a hike.

Wentworth Falls is one of the most popular waterfalls in the region. It cascades down from a high cliff, creating a stunning view and a refreshing mist.

The trail to the falls provides several lookout points, and for those who want to get closer, there's a steep path that leads to the bottom of the falls.

Another notable spot is **Govetts Leap,** a lookout that offers breathtaking views of the Grose Valley and the 180-meter-high Bridal Veil Falls.

Govetts Leap is a great location for photography, especially in the early morning or late afternoon when the light adds a soft glow to the cliffs and trees.

• **Indigenous Heritage and Cultural Sites**

The Blue Mountains are also rich in Indigenous heritage, with sites that have been significant to Indigenous Australians for thousands of years.

The Dharug and Gundungurra peoples are the traditional custodians of this land, and they have passed down stories and cultural practices through many generations.

One of the important sites in the Blue Mountains is the **Red Hands Cave,** which is located in the **Glenbrook** area.

The cave contains ancient handprints and stencils made by Indigenous people, believed to be thousands of years old.

These markings offer a glimpse into the lives of those who lived here long before European settlers arrived.

Visiting this site is a meaningful experience, as it allows visitors to connect with Australia's deep Indigenous history.

Many tours and experiences in the Blue Mountains are led by Indigenous guides, who share the stories, traditions, and connection to the land that have been part of their culture for centuries.

Learning from Indigenous guides can add a deeper understanding of the land and its history, giving visitors a new appreciation for the Blue Mountains.

• **Variety of plants and animals**

The Blue Mountains are home to a variety of plants and animals, many of which are unique to Australia.

In the forests, you'll find eucalyptus trees, along with native flowers like **waratahs and grevilleas**.

These plants provide food and shelter for a range of animals, including the **koala and greater glider**, which are often spotted in the eucalyptus trees.

Birdwatchers will enjoy the chance to see species like the **superb lyrebird**, known for its ability to mimic sounds, and the **yellow-tailed black cockatoo** with its striking yellow patches.

The Blue Mountains are also home to the **blue mountain water skink**, a rare and endangered lizard species found only in this region.

For those interested in wildlife, **Featherdale Wildlife Park** is nearby and provides a safe place to see animals up close, including kangaroos, wallabies, and wombats.

This park is a good option for families and anyone who wants to learn more about Australia's unique wildlife.

• Why Visit the Blue Mountains?

The Blue Mountains are special because they offer a mix of natural beauty, outdoor adventure, and cultural history.

Whether it's hiking to a scenic lookout, exploring ancient rock art, or just enjoying a picnic with views over the valley, there's something for everyone.

- Nature and Scenery

From the blue haze of the eucalyptus trees to stunning cliffs and waterfalls, the Blue Mountains offer some of Australia's most memorable landscapes.

- Outdoor Activities

Hiking, Scenic World rides, and walking through rainforests provide endless options for outdoor fun.

- Cultural Connection

The Blue Mountains are a place of deep cultural significance to Indigenous Australians, with many sites that highlight their rich history.

Hunter Valley

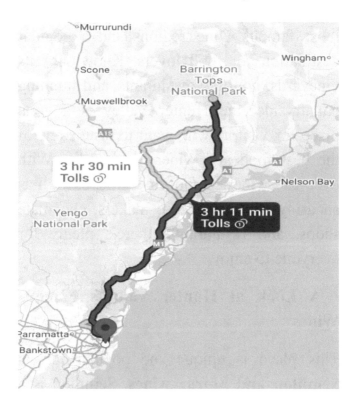

• **The map above shows distance (with time covered) from Sydney central to Hunter Valley**

Hunter Valley, located just two to three hours north of Sydney, is one of Australia's most famous wine regions and a popular destination for food lovers. Known for its vineyards, gourmet restaurants, and stunning countryside, the Hunter Valley is a great place for visitors who want to taste some of the best food and wine in Australia. With over 150 wineries and vineyards, as well as an array of local cheese makers, chocolate shops, and restaurants, there's plenty for everyone to enjoy.

• **A Look at Hunter Valley's Famous Wines**

This place is unique and popular for its **Semillon and Shiraz wines.** Semillon is a white wine with a light, fresh taste that can age well and develop unique flavors over time. Shiraz, on the other hand, is a rich, bold red wine known for its dark fruit flavors and smooth finish. Many of the vineyards here have been producing these wines for generations, and each winery offers a slightly different twist on these classic tastes.

One well-known winery in Hunter Valley is **Tyrrell's Wines.** Established in 1858, Tyrrell's is one of the oldest family-owned wineries in Australia. Their **Vat 1 Semillon** is considered one of the best examples of Hunter Valley Semillon, and visitors can sample it along with a variety of other wines in their tasting room. Another popular winery is **Brokenwood Wines**, famous for its **Graveyard Vineyard Shiraz**, which is bold and full-bodied.

• **The Experience of a Wine Tour**

Wine tours are one of the best ways to experience Hunter Valley. Most tours visit several wineries, allowing you to sample different wines and learn about the winemaking process. The tours usually begin with a walk through the vineyard, where guides explain how grapes are grown and harvested. Afterward, visitors get to see where the wine is produced, aged, and bottled before moving to the tasting room.

One highly-rated tour provider in Hunter Valley is **Two Fat Blokes Gourmet Tours.** This tour includes stops at several wineries, as well as a cheese-tasting experience, making it perfect for food and wine lovers. Another popular option is the **Hunter Valley Wine and Food Festival,** held every May and June. During the festival, wineries and restaurants across the valley host special tastings, dinners, and events, giving visitors a unique chance to enjoy the best flavors of the region.

• **Pairing Wine with Local Cheese and Chocolate**

In addition to wine, Hunter Valley is known for its high-quality cheeses and chocolates, which pair perfectly with the region's wines.

Binnorie Dairy is a popular spot for cheese lovers. They specialize in soft cheeses like **Marinated Feta and Brie,** which are creamy and flavorful. Visitors can sample their cheeses and learn about how they are made using local milk.

For a sweet treat, **Hunter Valley Chocolate Company** is a must-visit. They offer a wide range of handmade chocolates, from truffles to chocolate-covered nuts. Their **chocolate and wine pairing experience** is a favorite among visitors, as it combines the rich flavors of dark chocolate with the depth of local red wines. Trying different wines with chocolates and cheeses is a fun way to discover new flavors and see how well different tastes go together.

• **Gourmet Dining in Hunter Valley**

Hunter Valley's restaurants make the most of local ingredients, offering fresh, seasonal dishes that showcase the area's produce.

Some of the best-known restaurants are located within wineries, allowing visitors to enjoy fine dining surrounded by beautiful vineyards.

One popular dining spot is **Muse Restaurant,** located at **Hungerford Hill Winery.** Muse is known for its seasonal menus that feature local ingredients, such as freshly caught fish, vegetables, and herbs. The restaurant's focus is on simple, high-quality dishes that pair well with Hunter Valley wines. **Margan Restaurant,** located at Margan Winery, is another favorite. They grow many of their ingredients on-site in their garden, creating dishes that reflect the flavors of the region.

For a more casual experience, **The Cellar Restaurant** in Pokolbin offers a variety of dishes like pasta, salads, and wood-fired pizzas. Many of these meals are designed to complement local wines, allowing diners to enjoy a relaxed meal with a glass of Semillon or Shiraz.

• **Beyond Wine**

While wine tasting is the main attraction, Hunter Valley has other experiences that allow visitors to enjoy the beautiful landscape. A typical example of a famous activity here is hot air balloon ride. Companies like **Balloon Aloft** offer early morning flights over the vineyards and fields, giving visitors a bird's-eye view of the area as the sun rises. The view of the rolling hills and rows of vineyards from above is breathtaking, and the peaceful ride is a great way to start the day. After the balloon ride, many companies include a champagne breakfast, giving guests a chance to toast their adventure with a glass of sparkling wine.

• **Family-Friendly Activities**

Hunter Valley isn't just for adults. There are also plenty of family-friendly activities. **Hunter Valley Gardens** is a popular spot for visitors of all ages, featuring over 10 themed gardens, including an **Italian Grotto, Storybook Garden, and Sunken Garden.** The gardens are filled with colorful flowers, fountains, and sculptures, making them a fun place to explore and take photos.

For families with kids, the **Hunter Valley Wildlife Park** is a great choice. Here, visitors can see and even feed kangaroos, wallabies, and koalas. The park also has a variety of exotic animals, including lions and meerkats, making it an exciting stop for young travelers.

• **Planning Your Visit to Hunter Valley**

The best time to visit Hunter Valley is during autumn (March to May) and spring (September to November) when the weather is mild, and the vines are either changing color or in full bloom. However, each season offers its own charm. In the summer, vineyards are lush and green, while winter brings cooler temperatures, ideal for cozy wine tastings by the fire.

When planning a trip, keep in mind that weekends and holidays can be busy, so it's a good idea to book winery tours and restaurant reservations in advance. If you prefer a quieter experience, consider visiting mid-week, when there are fewer tourists.

Hunter Valley is accessible by car from Sydney, making it easy for a day trip or a weekend getaway. However, if you want to fully enjoy the wine-tasting experience, many visitors opt to stay overnight in one of the region's charming accommodations.

Options range from cozy cottages to luxury hotels, many of which are located on vineyard properties, offering scenic views and convenient access to wine tastings.

• Why Hunter Valley is Worth the Visit

Hunter Valley is an ideal destination for anyone interested in wine, food, and natural beauty.

It's a place where you can learn about the art of winemaking, taste award-winning wines, and enjoy delicious food, all while surrounded by stunning landscapes. With its family-friendly attractions, gourmet experiences, and wide range of outdoor activities, there's something for everyone in Hunter Valley.

Byron Bay and Beyond

Byron Bay is one of Australia's most famous beach towns, located on the northern coast of New South Wales.

Known for its laid-back vibe, beautiful beaches, and surf culture, Byron Bay is a favorite spot for travelers of all ages.

This town combines stunning natural beauty with a unique community feel, where locals and visitors come together to enjoy the beach, explore nearby nature, and relax in a peaceful setting.

From surfing lessons to scenic hikes and visiting nearby villages, there's so much to see and do in and around Byron Bay.

• **Beaches of Byron Bay**

Byron Bay is home to some of the best beaches in Australia, each with its own special features. **Main Beach** is the most popular beach in town, located close to Byron Bay's center. It's a great spot for families and those looking to relax by the water, with golden sand, calm waves, and lifeguards keeping an eye on things. It's also a good place for beginners to try surfing, as the waves here are usually gentle.

For those looking for a more adventurous surf spot, **The Pass** is the place to be.

Known for its long, rolling waves, The Pass attracts surfers from all over. You'll see surfers of all skill levels here, from beginners to experienced riders. It's a great beach to watch surfing if you're not ready to try it yourself, with a lookout area where you can watch the surfers ride the waves.

Another must-see beach is **Wategos Beach,** which is tucked in a bay near the famous Cape Byron Lighthouse. This beach is known for its calm waters and relaxed atmosphere, making it ideal for picnics and paddleboarding. Just past Wategos is **Little Wategos Beach,** the most easterly beach on mainland Australia. Little Wategos can only be reached by foot, but it's worth the walk for its secluded beauty and clear blue water.

• **Cape Byron Lighthouse**

One of the top things to do in Byron Bay is to visit **Cape Byron Lighthouse.** Perched on a high cliff, this iconic lighthouse offers some of the best views in the area. You can reach it by taking the **Cape Byron Walking Track**, a scenic trail that winds through coastal forests and along cliffs overlooking the ocean.

The walk to the lighthouse is around 3.7 kilometers (about 2.3 miles) round-trip and takes about 1-2 hours, depending on how many stops you make along the way. During migration season, which runs from June to November, you might even spot **humpback whales** from the cliffs. The lighthouse itself is a great spot to learn about the region's history and take in the sweeping views of the Pacific Ocean.

• **Surf Culture and Lessons in Byron Bay**

Byron Bay has a strong surf culture, and many people come here to experience surfing for the first time. If you're new to surfing, there are plenty of surf schools offering lessons for all ages and skill levels.

Let's Go Surfing is a popular surf school in Byron Bay, known for its friendly instructors and safe teaching methods. They provide surfboards, wetsuits, and everything you need, so all you have to bring is your enthusiasm.

For those who already know how to surf, Byron Bay offers a variety of waves to try. The town's beaches offer a mix of small waves for beginners and bigger waves for more experienced surfers. You'll see surfers carrying their boards through town, sharing tips, and chatting about the best spots. Surf shops like **Byron Bay Surf & Bike Hire** also make it easy to rent boards if you want to head out on your own.

• **Exploring Nearby Towns**

Byron Bay's charm extends beyond the beach, with nearby towns that offer unique experiences. Just a 15-minute drive from Byron Bay is the town of **Bangalow**. Known for its historic buildings and artistic community, Bangalow has a lovely main street lined with cafes, boutiques, and art galleries. The **Bangalow Market**, held on the fourth Sunday of every month, is a great place to find handmade crafts, local produce, and delicious food.

For a different kind of experience, take a trip to **Nimbin,** a small village about an hour's drive from Byron Bay. Nimbin is known for its alternative lifestyle and vibrant art scene. The town has a colorful atmosphere, with murals, sculptures, and a variety of shops selling art, crafts, and organic products. **The Nimbin Hemp Embassy** is a well-known spot in town where visitors can learn about the town's history and its unique approach to sustainable living.

• **Local Food and Markets**

Byron Bay is a great place to enjoy fresh, locally sourced food. Many of the restaurants and cafes here focus on organic and sustainable ingredients, offering dishes that are both delicious and healthy. **Three Blue Ducks** is a popular restaurant located on **The Farm**, a working farm just outside of town. Here, you can tour the farm, meet the animals, and enjoy a meal made from ingredients grown right on site.

Byron Bay also has several weekly markets, where locals and visitors come to buy fresh produce, handmade crafts, and more. The **Byron Bay Farmers Market** is held every Thursday morning and is a great place to sample fresh fruits, vegetables, and homemade treats. You'll find stalls selling everything from fresh bread to local honey, and there's often live music to enjoy as you browse.

Another popular event is the **Byron Community Market**, held on the first Sunday of each month. This market has a lively atmosphere, with stalls selling handmade jewelry, clothing, and art. Street performers and musicians add to the fun, making it a great way to spend a Sunday morning.

• **Outdoor Adventures Beyond the Beach**

While Byron Bay's beaches are its main attraction, the area also offers plenty of other outdoor activities. **Mount Warning, or Wollumbin,** is a popular spot for hiking. Located about an hour from Byron Bay, this ancient volcanic mountain offers a challenging but rewarding climb. The summit provides panoramic views of the surrounding area, and many people start the hike early to catch the sunrise from the top.

For a more relaxed outdoor experience, **Crystal Castle & Shambhala Gardens** is a beautiful retreat near Mullumbimby, about 20 minutes from Byron Bay. This peaceful garden is filled with giant crystals, tropical plants, and walking paths, making it a serene place to unwind. The gardens also host meditation sessions, workshops, and other activities that are open to visitors.

• **Festivals and Events in Byron Bay**

Byron Bay is known for its festivals, which attract visitors from all over the world. One of the biggest events is the **Byron Bay Bluesfest**, an annual music festival held over Easter weekend. Bluesfest features performances from international and Australian artists and covers a range of music styles, including blues, roots, and folk.

Another popular event is **Splendour in the Grass**, a music and arts festival held each July. This festival is known for its diverse lineup of artists and lively atmosphere, with performances, art installations, and plenty of food stalls. Splendour in the Grass is a favorite among young music fans and is one of Australia's largest music festivals.

• Why Byron Bay is a Must-Visit

Byron Bay's combination of beautiful beaches, relaxed atmosphere, and unique attractions makes it a special place to visit. Whether you're surfing at The Pass, hiking to Cape Byron Lighthouse, or exploring nearby villages like Bangalow, there's always something new to experience. The town's welcoming community, love for nature, and creative spirit make it easy to see why so many people fall in love with Byron Bay.

This beach town offers a bit of everything—sun, sand, culture, and nature. From enjoying fresh food at local markets to watching surfers catch waves, Byron Bay is a place where you can relax, have fun, and make memories.

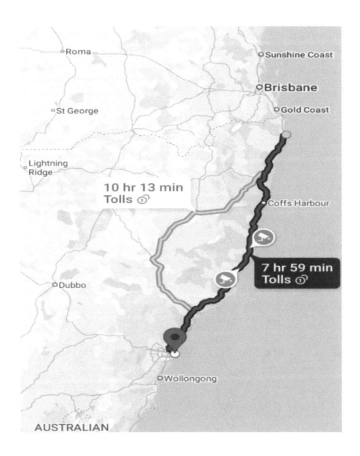

• The map above shows distance (with time covered) from Sydney central to Byron Bay

Chapter Three: The Great Barrier Reef and Queensland

The Great Barrier Reef

This place is located off the coast of Queensland, Australia. It's popularly known to be the largest coral reef system in the world today.

Stretching over 2,300 kilometers, this natural wonder is home to thousands of species of fish, coral, and marine life. The clear blue waters and colorful coral gardens make it a perfect place for snorkeling, diving, and reef tours. Whether you're a beginner or an experienced diver, there are plenty of spots on the reef that offer incredible underwater experiences.

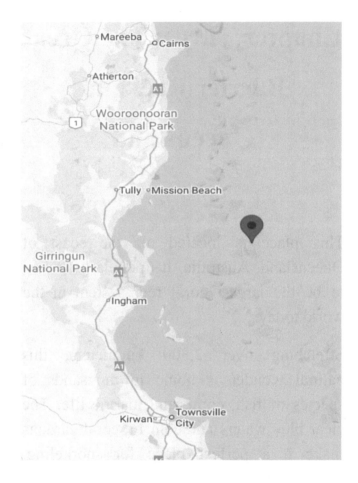

• The map above shows where the Great Barrier Reef is situated in Australia

Let's look at some of the best places to visit along the Great Barrier Reef, where you can explore this amazing marine world up close.

• **Top Spots for Snorkeling**

Snorkeling is a great way to see the reef without needing special equipment or training. With just a mask, snorkel, and fins, you can float above the coral and watch fish and other sea creatures below.

1. Green Island

Green Island is a beautiful coral cay located about 27 kilometers from Cairns. It's one of the easiest places to reach on the reef, making it a popular spot for families and beginners. The island has shallow waters, which means you can see the coral and marine life without going too deep. While snorkeling, you might spot giant clams, sea turtles, and colorful parrotfish. The waters around Green Island are also protected, so there's a lot of marine life to enjoy. Several companies, like **Big Cat Green Island Reef Cruises,** offer day trips to the island, including snorkeling gear and glass-bottom boat tours.

2. Fitzroy Island

Fitzroy Island is another beautiful spot near Cairns, just a 45-minute ferry ride away. This island has both soft sand beaches and coral beaches, giving you a variety of snorkeling spots to choose from. The water around the island is calm and clear, which makes it perfect for snorkeling. **Nudey Beach,** located on the island, is a top spot where you can snorkel right from the shore. It's common to see small reef sharks, rays, and schools of tropical fish here. Fitzroy Island Adventures offers tours that include ferry rides, snorkeling gear, and lunch packages.

3. Low Isles

Low Isles is a small, protected island about 15 kilometers from Port Douglas. This spot is known for its calm waters and colorful coral gardens, which are great for snorkeling.

Because it's a Marine National Park Zone, there are many types of fish, corals, and even sea turtles around the island. The reef here is shallow, so you don't have to go deep to see marine life. **Sailaway Port Douglas** offers eco-friendly sailing tours to the Low Isles, which include snorkeling tours with a guide who can help you identify the fish and coral.

• **Best Spots for Diving**

For those who want to go deeper, scuba diving offers a way to see parts of the reef that aren't visible from the surface.

The Great Barrier Reef has spots suitable for both beginners and experienced divers, with vibrant corals, caves, and marine creatures.

1. Cod Hole

Cod Hole is a famous dive site near Lizard Island, known for its large potato cod fish. These friendly fish are used to divers and will often swim right up to them, making for an exciting underwater experience. Besides the cod, you'll also see clownfish, angelfish, and sometimes even reef sharks. The dive site has excellent visibility, which means you can see the coral and fish clearly even at deeper levels. Liveaboard tours, like those by **Mike Ball Dive Expeditions,** offer trips to Cod Hole, giving divers the chance to explore this unique site over several days.

2. Ribbon Reefs

The Ribbon Reefs are located farther from the shore, stretching between Port Douglas and Lizard Island. They are a chain of 10 narrow reefs and are known for their healthy coral and diverse marine life.

These reefs are also great for spotting large species like the giant clams, sea turtles, and the Maori wrasse, a large and colorful fish. Some parts of the Ribbon Reefs are more challenging, so they're ideal for advanced divers. **Spirit of Freedom** offers multi-day trips that allow divers to explore multiple Ribbon Reefs, including night dives for those interested in seeing nocturnal marine life.

3. Osprey Reef

Osprey Reef is one of the most remote and stunning dive spots on the Great Barrier Reef. Located in the Coral Sea, it's famous for its crystal-clear water and dramatic walls that drop deep into the ocean. This site is best suited for advanced divers, as it's known for stronger currents and deeper dives.

At Osprey Reef, divers can encounter sharks, including reef sharks and even hammerheads. There are also huge coral formations and caves that make this a thrilling dive spot.

Pro Dive Cairns and Spirit of Freedom offer trips that include Osprey Reef as part of longer diving expeditions.

• **Reef Tours and Experiences**

For those who prefer to stay above the water or don't have experience snorkeling or diving, there are still plenty of ways to enjoy the beauty of the Great Barrier Reef. Many companies offer reef tours that include options like glass-bottom boat rides, semi-submersible submarines, and scenic helicopter flights.

1. Great Adventures Outer Reef Pontoon

Great Adventures operates a floating platform, or pontoon, on the Outer Reef, where visitors can spend the day experiencing the reef in different ways. From the pontoon, you can go snorkeling, ride in a semi-submersible submarine, or relax on the sun deck and enjoy the view. This pontoon is family-friendly, with activities for all ages, making it a great option if you're traveling with children. The platform even has an underwater observatory, so you can see marine life without getting wet.

2. Quicksilver Cruises to Agincourt Reef

Agincourt Reef is part of the Outer Reef and is known for its clear water and impressive coral formations. **Quicksilver Cruises** operates a large pontoon here, providing visitors with a variety of activities. You can go snorkeling, take an introductory dive, or ride in a glass-bottom boat. For those looking for an unforgettable experience, Quicksilver also offers scenic helicopter flights over the reef, giving you a bird's-eye view of the coral and ocean.

3. Helicopter and Seaplane Tours

For a different perspective of the Great Barrier Reef, a helicopter or seaplane tour offers a breathtaking view of the reef from above. The bright blue and green colors of the coral are most visible from the sky, and you can get a sense of how massive the reef system is.

Several companies, including **HeliTours North Queensland and GBR Helicopters,** offer scenic flights over famous sites like Heart Reef, a naturally heart-shaped coral formation. These tours are a fantastic way to see the reef's beauty, especially for those who prefer to stay dry.

• Protecting the Reef

The Great Barrier Reef is one of the most delicate ecosystems on Earth, and it faces threats from climate change, pollution, and coral bleaching.

Efforts are underway to protect and preserve the reef for future generations. Many tour operators in the region have taken steps to operate sustainably, ensuring that visitors can enjoy the reef responsibly.

For example, several companies follow eco-friendly practices, such as using environmentally friendly sunscreen, limiting the number of boats allowed in certain areas, and educating visitors about the importance of reef conservation.

When visiting the reef, it's important to follow guidelines to protect the environment. Simple steps like not touching the coral, avoiding single-use plastics, and using reef-safe sunscreen can make a big difference.

Many tours also include information sessions on how to interact with the reef in a way that doesn't harm the marine life or coral.

• **Why the Great Barrier Reef is a Must-Visit**

The Great Barrier Reef is one of the most beautiful and unique places on Earth. Its colorful coral, diverse marine life, and variety of activities make it a fantastic destination for all ages.

Whether you're snorkeling in the shallow waters around Green Island, diving with potato cod at Cod Hole, or taking in the view from a helicopter, there are so many ways to experience the reef.

It's a place where you can see nature up close, from tiny fish hiding in the coral to giant turtles swimming past. Visiting the reef also helps you understand the importance of protecting our natural world. With responsible travel and efforts to preserve the reef, we can ensure that this amazing underwater world remains vibrant and full of life for many years to come.

Cairns and Port Douglas

Cairns and Port Douglas are two popular cities in Queensland, Australia, that serve as gateways to some of the country's most amazing natural wonders—the Great Barrier Reef and the Daintree Rainforest. Located in the tropical far north, these cities are known for their warm weather, lush landscapes, and easy access to both the reef and the rainforest.

Whether you're interested in snorkeling, diving, or hiking through ancient forests, Cairns and Port Douglas offer exciting experiences for people of all ages.

• Cairns

Cairns is the larger of the two cities and is known for its lively vibe and endless outdoor activities. While it may not have its own sandy beaches (Cairns' coastline is mostly mudflats), the city has a famous **Esplanade Lagoon,** which is a large saltwater pool open to the public.

Locals and tourists alike love to visit this spot to swim, relax, and enjoy the view of the Coral Sea.

• **The Reef Fleet Terminal**

One of the main reasons people come to Cairns is to visit the Great Barrier Reef. The **Reef Fleet Terminal** in Cairns is where many reef tours begin. There are numerous tour companies based here, such as **Quicksilver Cruises and Reef Magic Cruises,** which offer a range of experiences, from snorkeling trips to scenic helicopter rides over the reef.

For those new to snorkeling or diving, many tours offer lessons and guided experiences. Some tours also have glass-bottom boats for those who prefer to stay dry while still seeing the underwater world.

• **The Kuranda Scenic Railway & Skyrail Rainforest Cableway (A beautiful location)**

Apart from the reef, Cairns is also close to the stunning rainforest town of **Kuranda**.

Visitors can take the **Kuranda Scenic Railway** up through the mountains, enjoying beautiful views of the rainforest, rivers, and waterfalls along the way. The journey ends in Kuranda, where there are markets, shops, and the **Australian Butterfly Sanctuary**.

For a different way down, the **Skyrail Rainforest Cableway** offers a bird's-eye view of the rainforest, with stops at scenic lookouts.

This trip is especially popular for families as it combines both adventure and learning about the rainforest.

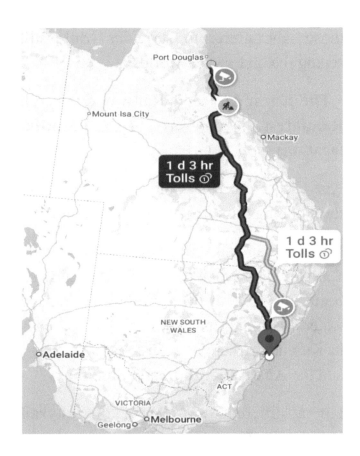

- **The map above shows distance (with time covered) from Sydney central to Cairns**

• **Cairns Night Markets**

In the evenings, Cairns' **Night Markets** come alive, with a variety of stalls selling everything from souvenirs to street food.

Located on the Esplanade, this market is a great place to try local snacks, shop for unique gifts, and experience the friendly atmosphere of Cairns.

You can find items like didgeridoos, boomerangs, and handmade jewelry that make for memorable keepsakes.

• **Port Douglas**

Port Douglas, about an hour's drive north of Cairns, is a smaller town with a relaxed vibe. While it's smaller than Cairns, Port Douglas has its own special charm and attracts visitors looking for a quieter place to stay.

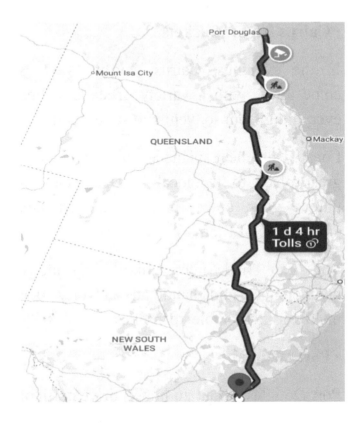

- The map above shows distance (with time covered) from Sydney central to Port Douglas

The drive between Cairns and Port Douglas along the **Captain Cook Highway** is itself a highlight, as it offers stunning ocean views and scenic lookouts along the way.

• **Four Mile Beach**

This is one of the main attractions we have in Port Douglas. This long stretch of golden sand is ideal for walking, sunbathing, and swimming. Unlike Cairns, where the coastline is mostly mudflats, Port Douglas has a proper sandy beach with calm waters that are perfect for families. In the summer months, a swimming area with stinger nets is set up to protect swimmers from jellyfish, making it safe to enjoy the water year-round.

• **Macrossan Street**

Macrossan Street is the main street in Port Douglas, lined with cafes, shops, and restaurants.

Here, visitors can find everything from art galleries to boutiques selling beachwear. It's a lovely place to take a stroll, enjoy some ice cream, or have a meal at one of the many outdoor restaurants. A popular spot here is **Salsa Bar & Grill**, known for its fresh seafood and relaxed vibe.

• **Wildlife Habitat Port Douglas**

If you're interested in Australian wildlife, **Wildlife Habitat Port Douglas** is a great place to visit.

This animal park offers visitors the chance to see native animals like kangaroos, koalas, and even crocodiles up close. They also offer a "Breakfast with the Birds" experience, where guests can enjoy a meal while colorful tropical birds fly around the dining area.

• The Daintree Rainforest

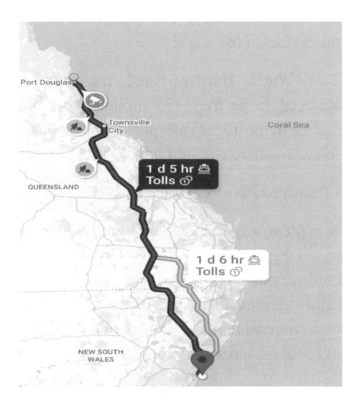

• The map above shows distance (with time covered) from Sydney central to Daintree Rainforest

Both Cairns and Port Douglas are close to the **Daintree Rainforest,** one of the oldest rainforests in the world.

This World Heritage-listed rainforest is believed to be over 135 million years old and is home to unique plants and animals found nowhere else on Earth.

• Daintree River Cruise

A popular way to experience the Daintree is by taking a **Daintree River Cruise.** These guided boat tours give you a chance to see saltwater crocodiles, one of the area's most famous residents, as well as other wildlife like snakes, birds, and frogs.

The tours also provide information about the river and the ecosystem, making it both fun and educational.

• Mossman Gorge

Another must-visit spot in the Daintree is **Mossman Gorge.** Located just 20 minutes from Port Douglas, Mossman Gorge has clear, freshwater pools where visitors can swim and relax.

There are walking trails through the rainforest, and guided tours led by the **Kuku Yalanji people,** the traditional owners of the land, offer insights into the cultural and spiritual significance of the area.

The guided tours also teach visitors about bush foods, medicines, and traditional rainforest knowledge.

• **Cape Tribulation**

Cape Tribulation is where the Daintree Rainforest meets the Great Barrier Reef, making it one of the only places in the world where two World Heritage sites come together.

The beaches here are beautiful, and there are boardwalks that take you through the rainforest and out to viewpoints overlooking the ocean.

Cape Tribulation is a great place for nature lovers, with many opportunities for birdwatching, hiking, and spotting wildlife.

- **Choosing Between Cairns and Port Douglas**

Many travelers wonder whether to stay in Cairns or Port Douglas. Both places offer unique experiences, and your choice may depend on what kind of trip you're looking for.

- **Cairns** is the place to go if you want a lively atmosphere with lots of options for activities and tours. It's a bustling city with plenty of restaurants, shops, and nightlife.

Plus, it's closer to Kuranda and has easy access to the Reef Fleet Terminal for Great Barrier Reef tours.

- **Port Douglas,** on the other hand, is a more relaxed, beachside town. It's perfect for those who want a quieter stay while still having access to the reef and the rainforest.

Port Douglas is also closer to the Daintree Rainforest and offers beautiful beaches, making it ideal for those who enjoy spending time by the ocean.

• **Getting Around**

Getting between Cairns and Port Douglas is easy, with several transport options available.

You can rent a car, which gives you the freedom to explore at your own pace, or take a shuttle service like the **Exemplar Coaches and Limousines.**

The drive along the Captain Cook Highway is scenic, with views of the Coral Sea and lush rainforest, and only takes about an hour. Some visitors choose to stay in both Cairns and Port Douglas to experience the best of both worlds.

Gold Coast

The **Gold Coast** is one of the most famous destinations in Queensland, Australia, known for its stunning beaches, thrilling theme parks, and exciting nightlife. Located just south of Brisbane, the Gold Coast is a place where both families and young adults can have a blast. Whether you're into surfing, amusement parks, or enjoying the vibrant nightlife, the Gold Coast offers a little bit of everything.

• **Beaches**

The Gold Coast is famous for its beautiful beaches, making it a popular spot for beach lovers and surfers. With over 40 kilometers of coastline, you'll find plenty of golden sand and rolling waves to enjoy.

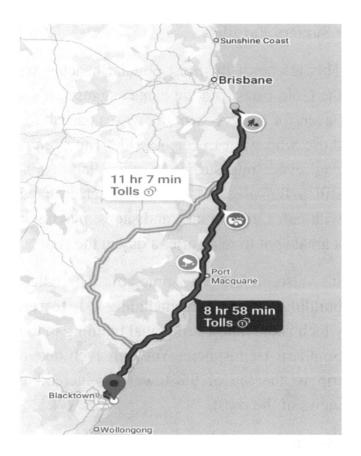

• **The map above shows distance (with time covered) from Sydney central to Gold Coast**

• **Surfers Paradise**

This is one of the most popular beaches on the Gold Coast. As the name suggests, it's a haven for surfers, with big waves perfect for those who want to catch a ride. But even if you're not into surfing, Surfers Paradise is still a fun place to be. The beach is lined with cafes, restaurants, and shops, making it a great spot to relax after a day in the sun.

It's also home to some of the tallest buildings in the area, including **Q1 Tower,** which is the tallest residential building in the Southern Hemisphere. You can even take a trip to the top of the tower for incredible views of the coast.

• **Burleigh Heads**

If you're looking for a quieter spot, **Burleigh Heads** is a perfect option. This beach has a laid-back vibe and is known for its beautiful parkland and excellent surf breaks.

The nearby **Burleigh Head National Park** offers scenic walking trails through rainforests and along cliffs, providing fantastic views of the beach and the ocean.

This is a great place to enjoy nature and escape the hustle and bustle of more touristy areas.

• **Coolangatta**

At the southern end of the Gold Coast is **Coolangatta,** another beautiful beach with calm waters that are perfect for swimming. This area is known for its relaxed atmosphere and less crowded beaches, making it ideal for families and those looking to unwind.

• **Theme Parks**

It's good you know that in Australia, the Gold Coast has some of best theme parks you can find anywhere. Whether you're looking for heart-pounding roller coasters or opportunities to meet your favorite characters, the Gold Coast has something for everyone.

• **Dreamworld**

Dreamworld is one of the most popular theme parks on the Gold Coast. It has a wide range of attractions for all ages. There are thrilling roller coasters, including **The Tower of Terror and The Giant Drop,** as well as gentler rides for younger visitors.

Dreamworld is also home to **Corroboree,** an area where you can experience Indigenous Australian culture, and Tiger **Island,** where you can see and learn about the park's famous tigers.

• **Warner Bros. Movie World**

For movie buffs, **Warner Bros. Movie World** is the place to go. This park brings Hollywood to life with exciting rides based on famous movies and TV shows.

Fans of superheroes will love the **Justice League 3D ride,** while those looking for thrills can take on the **Green Lantern Coaster or Superman Escape,** both of which offer high-speed fun. There are also live shows and parades featuring popular characters like Batman, Wonder Woman, and Bugs Bunny.

• **Sea World**

If you're more into marine life, **SeaWorld** is the perfect spot. This park combines both theme park attractions and a marine animal experience. You can enjoy rides like the **Storm Coaster** or watch dolphins, seals, and even polar bears in action.

Sea World is also a great place for learning about ocean conservation and the incredible creatures that call the sea their home.

• **Wet'n'Wild Gold Coast**

For water park enthusiasts, **Wet'n'Wild** is the place to cool off. This water park is packed with thrilling water slides, lazy rivers, and wave pools.

The park has a variety of slides that range from gentle to adrenaline-pumping, including the **Kamikaze,** one of the most exciting water slides in the world. It's a fun way to spend a hot day with friends and family.

• **Nightlife**

When the sun sets, the Gold Coast comes alive with vibrant nightlife. From trendy beach clubs to relaxed bars, there's no shortage of places to enjoy a night out.

• **Surfers Paradise Nightlife**

Surfers Paradise is at the heart of the Gold Coast's nightlife scene. This area has a wide variety of bars, clubs, and lounges.

One popular spot is **The Island Rooftop**, a rooftop bar with beautiful views of the city and beach.

Another favorite is **SinCity Nightclub,** known for its high-energy music and dancing. Whether you're into casual drinks or dancing all night, Surfers Paradise has something for everyone.

• **Broadbeach**

A bit more relaxed than Surfers Paradise, **Broadbeach** has a more laid-back vibe but still offers plenty of options for nightlife.

You can grab a cocktail at a local bar like **The Star Gold Coast,** which is both a casino and entertainment venue with restaurants, bars, and live music.

The area is also home to **Kurrawa Surf Club**, which is a great place for a more relaxed evening with a cold drink and delicious food.

• Coolangatta

For a quieter night out, head to **Coolangatta.** It's not as busy as other parts of the Gold Coast, but it offers a more laid-back atmosphere with beachside bars and local cafes.

You can enjoy a drink with a view of the beach, or grab some fresh seafood at one of the restaurants.

• Shopping and Dining

The Gold Coast is also a great place for shopping and dining.

From upscale shopping centers to casual markets, there are plenty of options to satisfy your shopping needs.

• Pacific Fair Shopping Centre

One of the biggest shopping malls on the Gold Coast is **Pacific Fair**, located in Broadbeach.

This center has everything from high-end fashion stores to local boutiques, so you can shop for just about anything.

There's also a large food court and several sit-down restaurants offering a variety of cuisines, from Australian to Asian.

• **Chevron Renaissance Shopping Centre**

Another popular shopping spot is **Chevron Renaissance,** located in the heart of Surfers Paradise.

This shopping center offers everything from fashion to home goods, and it's also home to some great dining options. If you're looking for something more local, visit the **Carrara Markets** for a mix of fresh produce, crafts, and unique souvenirs.

• **Eating on the Gold Coast**

When it comes to food, the Gold Coast has something for every taste. In Surfers Paradise, you can enjoy a seafood feast at

Hurricane's Grill or try a famous Australian meat pie at **The Pie Place.**

Broadbeach is home to many restaurants offering international cuisines, including Italian, Japanese, and Thai. The Gold Coast also has an abundance of cafes serving fresh, local produce, making it a food lover's paradise.

• **Getting Around the Gold Coast**

The Gold Coast has a well-developed public transportation system, including buses and the **G:link tram.** The tram runs from **Broadbeach to Helensvale,** making it easy to get around the main areas. If you're planning to visit the theme parks, there are buses that go directly to places like Dreamworld, Sea World, and Movie World. For more flexibility, you can rent a car, which is a great way to explore the area at your own pace.

Brisbane

Brisbane is the capital of Queensland, Australia, and is often called the "River City" because of the beautiful Brisbane River that flows right through its heart. The city has a mix of modern attractions, cultural spots, and plenty of outdoor activities. Whether you're exploring the lively South Bank, enjoying the art scene, or taking in the stunning views along the river, Brisbane offers something for everyone.

• **Brisbane River**

The **Brisbane River** is one of the city's biggest features, and there are many ways to enjoy it. You can take a relaxing ferry ride along the river to see some of the best views of the city, or you could hop on a **CityCat** ferry, which is a fast, affordable way to travel between different parts of Brisbane.

The ferries are a great way to see the city from the water and take in the skyline, parks, and bridges.

Another popular way to enjoy the river is by taking a **kayak or stand-up paddleboard.** For those who enjoy more adventure, kayaking lets you paddle right along the river and see parts of Brisbane from a unique perspective. There are also plenty of walking paths along the river where you can take a peaceful stroll, jog, or bike ride while watching the boats go by.

The **Story Bridge** is known to be one of the most popular and beautiful landmarks in Brisbane. This bridge connects the northern and southern parts of the city, and it's a popular spot for photos. If you're up for an adventure, you can do the **Story Bridge Adventure Climb,** which takes you to the top for amazing views of the city and the surrounding areas.

• South Bank

One of the most fun and relaxing places to visit in Brisbane is **South Bank.**

This area is located just across the river from the city center and has everything you need for a great day out, including parks, cultural spots, and food options.

• South Bank Parklands

At the heart of South Bank is the **South Bank Parklands,** a beautiful park that has lots of green spaces, gardens, and walking paths. It's a great place to have a picnic, play games, or just relax. One of the park's most popular spots is the **Streets Beach,** a man-made beach with sand, a lagoon, and even lifeguards. It's perfect for a swim if you don't want to go to the ocean but still want that beach feeling.

If you're visiting with kids, the **Wheel of Brisbane** is a giant Ferris wheel located at

South Bank. You can hop on for a ride and get a bird's-eye view of the city. It's a great way to see the Brisbane skyline and the river from above.

• **Cultural Attractions**

South Bank is also home to some of Brisbane's top cultural spots. The **Queensland Art Gallery and the Gallery of Modern Art (GOMA)** are located here, both of which showcase a variety of artworks from local and international artists. You can explore paintings, sculptures, and even interactive art exhibits. GOMA is especially known for its contemporary art and often has fun, hands-on exhibits that kids and adults alike will enjoy.

The **Queensland Museum and Sciencentre** is another popular attraction at South Bank. It's an interactive museum that covers a range of topics from dinosaurs to space exploration. If you're curious about how the world works, the Sciencentre has lots of fun exhibits that make learning feel like an adventure.

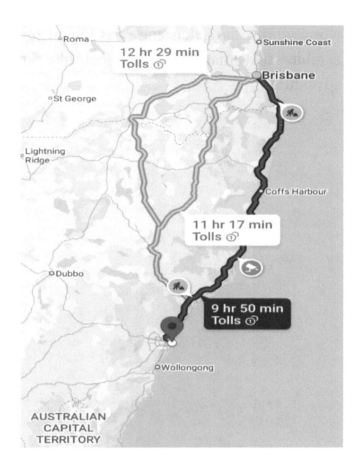

• The map above shows distance (with time covered) from Sydney central to Queensland Museum and Sciencentre

• **Enjoy a favorite food and drink, and also Shop at South Bank**

South Bank is also full of places to eat, drink, and shop. The **South Bank Collective Markets** offer a range of local handmade products, food, and live music on weekends.

For a nice meal, you can check out **Popolo,** an Italian restaurant that overlooks the river, or **The Collective,** which has a wide selection of food from different kitchens.

If you're in the mood for dessert, **Max Brenner** serves delicious chocolate treats, perfect for a sweet ending to your day.

• **Brisbane's Arts and Culture Scene**

Brisbane has a strong arts and culture scene that attracts visitors from all over the world.

The city is home to a variety of theaters, galleries, and festivals that showcase local talent and bring in international acts.

- **Queensland Performing Arts Centre (QPAC)**

One of the main places to experience live performances in Brisbane is the **Queensland Performing Arts Centre (QPAC).** Located at South Bank, QPAC hosts a variety of shows, from plays and musicals to ballet and orchestras. If you love the arts, catching a show at QPAC is a must-do. The center's stunning architecture also makes it a great place to explore before or after a performance.

- **Brisbane Powerhouse**

Another popular venue for the arts is the **Brisbane Powerhouse**, an old power station that has been transformed into a cultural hub. This space hosts theater productions, comedy shows, and live music performances. The Powerhouse is located right by the river, so you can enjoy the views of the water while you take in a show.

It's also home to a café and restaurant where you can grab a bite to eat.

• Street Art and Public Installations

Brisbane is known for its street art scene, with murals and installations scattered throughout the city. The **Woolloongabba** neighborhood is home to some of the best street art, with large murals covering the walls of buildings. You can also spot public art installations around South Bank and in various parks across Brisbane. If you enjoy art, take a walking tour through the city to see these vibrant creations up close.

• Festivals and Events

Brisbane is a city that loves its festivals. Every year, the city hosts major events like the **Brisbane Festival,** which features theater, music, and dance performances. Another favorite is **The Ekka**, the Royal Queensland Show, which celebrates agriculture, food, and family fun with rides, animals, and entertainment. There's also the **Brisbane International Film Festival,** where you can catch a variety of films from around the world.

• **Shopping and Dining in Brisbane**

Brisbane is also a great place to shop and enjoy delicious food. The **Queen Street Mall** is the city's main shopping street, where you can find big-name brands, department stores, and local boutiques. If you're into fashion, Queen Street is where you'll want to be. For more unique finds, visit the **James Street** area, known for its trendy stores and cafes.

When it comes to dining, Brisbane has a wide range of options. If you're in the mood for fresh seafood, head to **The Fishery** in the **Eagle Street Pier** area, where you can enjoy beautiful views of the river while eating. For something more casual, try **Eat Street Northshore,** a food market offering everything from pizza to sushi, all in a lively setting with live music.

• Getting Around Brisbane

Brisbane has an excellent public transport system that makes it easy to get around. The city is well connected by **buses, trains,** and the **CityCat ferries.** You can buy an **Opal card or a GoCard,** which allows you to use all forms of public transport. The **CityCycle** bike hire program is also a great option for those who want to explore the city on two wheels.

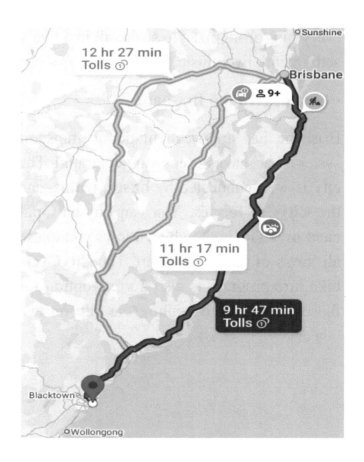

- The map above shows distance (with time covered) from Sydney central to Brisbane

Whitsunday Islands

- **The map above shows Whitsunday Islands**

These are a group of seventy four islands. They are located off the beautiful coast of Queensland. These islands are famous for their white sandy beaches, crystal-clear waters, and lush tropical landscapes. If you're looking for a tropical getaway, the Whitsundays offer the perfect place to relax, have fun, and enjoy the beautiful surroundings.

• **Whitehaven Beach**

This is one of the most beautiful and popular attractions we have in the Whitsundays. This beach is often called one of the most beautiful beaches in the world. What makes it so special is its pure white sand, made from 98% silica, which gives it a soft, powdery feel. The sand is so fine that it doesn't get hot under the sun, making it comfortable to walk on barefoot all day.

Whitehaven Beach stretches for about seven kilometers along **Whitsunday Island,** the largest of the islands in the group. The beach is surrounded by crystal-clear waters that are perfect for swimming and relaxing. It's also a great spot for a picnic, with plenty of places to relax under the shade of trees while enjoying the views.

To reach Whitehaven Beach, you can take a boat tour from **Airlie Beach**, the main gateway to the Whitsundays. Many tours also include a stop at **Hill Inlet,** which is a short walk from the beach. From the viewpoint at Hill Inlet, you can see an amazing sight: the white sand of Whitehaven Beach swirling with turquoise water, creating beautiful patterns. This view is one of the most photographed scenes in the Whitsundays.

• **Sailing Adventures**

The Whitsunday Islands are famous for their sailing opportunities. The calm, clear waters and the warm weather make the area a popular destination for sailing. Whether you're an experienced sailor or someone who just wants to try it out, there are many ways to enjoy the experience.

If you've always wanted to try sailing, you can join a day sailing tour. These tours are guided by experienced captains who will take you around the islands. You can spend the day on a **luxury yacht,** enjoying the gentle breeze while cruising through the beautiful waters. Some tours even offer snorkeling stops at coral reefs, where you can swim with colorful fish and see marine life up close.

For those who prefer a more adventurous experience, you can try an overnight sailing tour. These tours take you on a multi-day adventure through the Whitsundays, where you can sleep on board the boat and enjoy the peacefulness of the islands at night. Some overnight tours even include a visit to **Hamilton Island,** a popular resort island known for its great beaches, restaurants, and fun activities.

For people with more sailing experience, you can rent a bareboat (a boat without a crew) and sail the Whitsundays on your own. There are companies that will teach you everything you need to know about handling a boat, and then you can set out to explore the islands at your own pace.

• **Island Hopping**

While Whitehaven Beach is the most famous, the Whitsunday Islands have many other beautiful places to visit. If you're up for some island hopping, you can explore a variety of islands, each with its own charm.

• **Hamilton Island**

Hamilton Island is one of the largest and most popular islands in the Whitsundays. It has a wide range of accommodations, from luxury resorts to more affordable options.

The island is great for families, with activities like go-kart racing, mini-golf, and paddleboarding. If you're a nature lover, you can take a walk up **One Tree Hill** for an amazing view of the Whitsundays and the surrounding waters. The island also has a beautiful beach called **Catseye Beach,** where you can swim, snorkel, and relax.

• **Daydream Island**

Daydream Island is another popular destination in the Whitsundays. It has stunning beaches, a **swimming lagoon, and a reef lagoon** where you can snorkel and see tropical fish. The island is also home to the **Daydream Island Resort,** which has a **living reef**—a coral lagoon where you can get a close-up view of marine life without getting in the water.

• **Long Island**

Long Island is known for its hiking trails, quiet beaches, and relaxing atmosphere.

Unlike some of the more touristy islands, Long Island offers a peaceful getaway. You can take a walk through the **Long Island National Park** and see native wildlife, including wallabies and birds. It's also a great spot for picnics and barbecues, with areas set up for guests to enjoy the beautiful natural surroundings.

• **Whitsunday Islands National Park**

Many of the Whitsunday Islands are part of the **Whitsunday Islands National Park,** which helps protect the area's natural beauty. The park includes several smaller islands, and visitors can explore them through hiking, birdwatching, and other outdoor activities. The park is also home to a variety of wildlife, including seabirds, lizards, and marine animals like sea turtles and dolphins.

• **Water Sports**

Besides sailing, the waters around the Whitsunday Islands offer plenty of opportunities for other water sports. **Snorkeling and scuba diving** are popular activities, thanks to the area's proximity to the Great Barrier Reef. There are several tour companies that take visitors to the reef, where you can snorkel in the crystal-clear waters and see colorful coral reefs and marine life.

If you're an experienced diver, you can join a **scuba diving tour** that takes you to deeper parts of the reef. There are many dive sites around the Whitsundays, including the **Blue Pearl Bay** on Hayman Island, known for its incredible coral gardens and the chance to see giant clams, stingrays, and schools of fish.

• **When to Visit the Whitsundays**

May to October is the most ideal period to visit the place. This is when the weather is sunny and warm, with less chance of rain. The waters are calm, and it's perfect for sailing, snorkeling, and other outdoor activities. The wet season (from November to April) can bring more rain and warmer temperatures, but it's still possible to visit during this time if you prefer a quieter experience with fewer crowds.

Chapter Four: Uluru, Outback, and Northern Territory Adventures

Uluru (Ayers Rock)

Uluru is also referred to as the Ayers Rock. It's famously known to be one of the most popular landmarks in Australia.

Located in the heart of the **Northern Territory** in the **Outback,** this giant red rock stands 348 meters tall and is about 9.4 kilometers around its base.

It's a sacred place for the **Anangu,** the Aboriginal people of the area, and a symbol of Australia's natural beauty. Visiting Uluru is a chance to learn about Aboriginal culture, experience stunning views, and see one of the most amazing art installations in the world.

• **The Cultural Significance of Uluru**

Uluru has been a place of great significance to the **Anangu people** for thousands of years. For the Anangu, Uluru is not just a rock—it's a living part of their culture, history, and spirituality. According to Anangu beliefs, the land, including Uluru, was created by ancestors during the **Tjukurpa,** or Dreamtime, which is the Aboriginal understanding of the world's creation.

The rock is filled with ancient cave paintings, carvings, and stories that tell the history of the Anangu people. Visitors to Uluru can learn about these stories through guided tours led by Anangu guides. These tours help people understand the deep connection the Anangu have with Uluru and the surrounding land.

One of the most important cultural aspects of Uluru is that it is sacred to the Anangu. The rock is part of their spiritual beliefs, and for many years, the Anangu have asked visitors not to climb it, as it is a significant site in their traditions. Today, climbing Uluru is no longer allowed to show respect for the wishes of the traditional owners.

• **Sunset Views**

One of the best things to do at Uluru is to watch the sunset. As the sun sets behind the rock, it creates a stunning visual display. The color of Uluru changes from deep red to bright orange, purple, and pink, reflecting the changing light. It's a magical moment, and many people gather at the Uluru sunset viewing area to take in the view.

The changing colors of Uluru are caused by the way the light hits the rock's surface. The rock is made from a type of sandstone that contains iron oxide, which gives it its red color. As the sun moves across the sky, it creates different angles of light, making the rock seem to glow. This is a must-see experience for anyone visiting the area, and it's a chance to take some amazing photos.

It's also worth visiting in the early morning to catch the sunrise over Uluru. The sunrise, like the sunset, brings a new light to the rock, making it look even more beautiful in the early morning glow. Many visitors enjoy both the sunrise and sunset to fully experience the changing colors of this iconic landmark.

• **The Field of Light Art Installation**

One of the newest attractions near Uluru is the **Field of Light**, an art installation created by British artist **Bruce Munro.** This installation consists of over 50,000 solar-powered lights that illuminate the desert landscape at night. The lights are arranged in patterns that resemble flowers and create a beautiful scene against the backdrop of Uluru.

Field of Light is located in the desert just outside the Uluru-Kata Tjuta National Park. Visitors can walk through the glowing display, which is open every night. The lights change color and slowly fade in and out, creating an ethereal, almost magical atmosphere. The best time to visit the Field of Light is after the sun has set and the sky is dark. It's a peaceful and awe-inspiring experience that offers a different way to experience the beauty of the Outback.

The installation is not just a beautiful display of lights; it also has a deeper meaning. It's a way to connect the natural world with human creativity, as well as to honor the land and culture of the Anangu people. The light installation has become a popular way for people to experience Uluru in a new and unique way, offering a contrast to the more traditional views of the rock at sunrise and sunset.

• **Kata Tjuta**

While Uluru is the most famous landmark in the area, there is another stunning natural feature nearby: **Kata Tjuta (also known as The Olgas).** Kata Tjuta is a group of large, domed rock formations located about 50 kilometers west of Uluru.

Kata Tjuta is made up of 36 domes, and the rock formations are even older than Uluru. They are made of a different type of rock and have a unique appearance. Visitors can take a walk through the **Valley of the Winds,** one of the best hiking trails in the area. This trail takes you through the stunning rock formations, offering spectacular views of the surrounding desert and the distant horizon.

Another popular spot at Kata Tjuta is the **Walpa Gorge** walk, a shorter and easier trail that takes you through the gorge between the domes. The paths through Kata Tjuta provide a chance to see some of the unique plant and animal life of the desert, including species that are only found in this part of Australia.

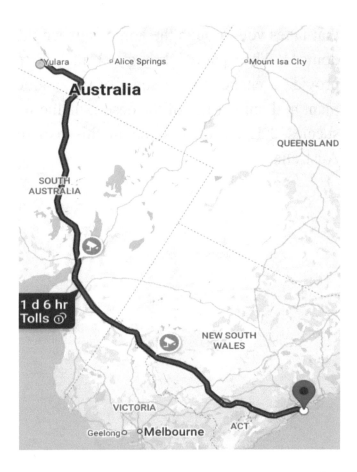

- The map above shows distance (with time covered) from Sydney central to Uluru

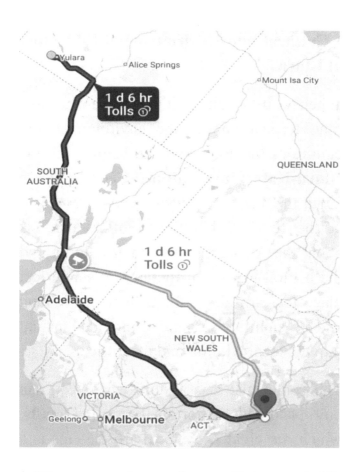

• The map above shows distance (with time covered) from Sydney central to Kata Tjuta

• **Cultural and Environmental Education at Uluru**

When visiting Uluru, it's important to take time to learn about the environment and culture of the area. You can begin from the **Uluru-Kata Tjuta Cultural Centre** to learn about the place. This visitor center is located at the base of Uluru and offers exhibits about the Anangu people, their culture, and the natural history of the area. It's a perfect place to learn about the history of the land and its significance, and it provides insight into the local wildlife and plant life.

The center also has a store where you can buy handmade Aboriginal art and crafts, which are created by local artists. This is a great way to take home a piece of the culture and support the local community.

• **Visiting Uluru and Its Surroundings**

The best time you need to consider visiting should be between April and October. The weather in the Outback can get extremely hot during the summer, so it's better to visit during the fall or spring when the temperatures are more comfortable for outdoor activities.

If you're staying in the area, there are several accommodations near Uluru, ranging from camping and eco-lodges to luxury resorts. One popular place to stay is the **Sails in the Desert** hotel, which offers a comfortable and relaxing environment after a day of sightseeing.

There are also several guided tours available, including Camel Rides at sunset, where you can ride a camel across the desert and watch the changing colors of Uluru. Helicopter tours are another option if you want to see Uluru and Kata Tjuta from the air.

Alice Springs

Alice Springs, located in the heart of **Australia's Outback**, is a town full of adventure, history, and unique desert landscapes. As one of the most well-known places in the **Northern Territory**, it offers a mix of cultural experiences, outdoor activities, and a chance to learn about the land's history. Whether you're visiting for the natural beauty, the wildlife, or to explore Aboriginal culture, Alice Springs has something for everyone.

• The Desert Landscapes of Alice Springs

The first thing you notice when you arrive in Alice Springs is the vast desert landscape that surrounds the town. The area is part of the **Red Centre,** known for its wide, flat plains, rocky hills, and red sandy soil. The desert is full of life, even though it might look empty at first glance. Animals like kangaroos, dingoes, and even camels roam the land, while a variety of birds, including parrots and eagles, can be spotted soaring above.

One of the most famous natural spots near Alice Springs is **Simpsons Gap.** Just a short drive from the town, it's a beautiful place where you can see the stunning contrast of tall cliffs against the dry riverbed below. The area is also home to black-footed rock wallabies, which you can sometimes spot hopping around the rocky terrain.

Another must-visit spot is **West MacDonnell National Park**, which stretches over 160 kilometers. This park is filled with beautiful gorges, waterholes, and walking trails. One of the most popular places in the park is **Ormiston Gorge**, where you can swim in a natural waterhole surrounded by the red cliffs of the desert. It's a peaceful spot, perfect for a cool dip on a hot day.

• Aboriginal Culture and History

Alice Springs is also an important center for **Aboriginal culture**. The town is located on Arrernte land, and the **Arrernte people** have lived in the region for thousands of years. Their connection to the land is deep and spiritual, and the area around Alice Springs is filled with **sacred sites** and stories that have been passed down through generations.

One of the best ways to learn about the culture of the local Aboriginal people is to visit the **Araluen Cultural Precinct.** This site includes art galleries, museums, and performance spaces where you can discover more about the history, traditions, and art of the **Arrernte** people and other Aboriginal groups from the region. The **Araluen Arts Centre** is home to some of the most famous Aboriginal art in Australia, and the galleries showcase colorful paintings, sculptures, and more that tell stories of the land, animals, and people.

The **Alice Springs Desert Park** is another great place to learn about Aboriginal culture. Here, you can walk through different desert habitats and learn how the local people have used the land for survival. The park offers interactive exhibits where you can learn about Aboriginal bush foods, medicines, and how traditional tools are made and used. You can also watch live performances and shows that bring these ancient traditions to life.

• **Camel Tours**

One of the most fun and unique ways to explore the desert around Alice Springs is on a camel ride. Camels were introduced to Australia in the 19th century and quickly became an important mode of transport across the desert. Today, camels are a big part of the landscape, and taking a camel tour is one of the best ways to see the desert from a different perspective.

There are several companies that offer camel tours, such as **The Alice Springs Desert Park Camel Ride.** These tours take you through the red desert sands, where you can experience the quiet beauty of the landscape while riding atop one of these gentle animals. You'll get to see some of the same sights that early explorers and traders might have seen, traveling across the Outback by camel. The tours usually include a guide who shares information about the history of camels in Australia, as well as the plants and animals in the desert.

Camel rides are a great way to learn about the harsh yet beautiful desert environment, and many tours take place in the early morning or late afternoon, when the temperatures are cooler and the desert light is perfect for taking photographs.

• **Alice Springs**

While the landscapes and culture are a big part of what makes Alice Springs so special, the town itself is also full of things to do. **Todd Mall**, the main street in Alice Springs, is lined with shops, cafes, and galleries. It's a great place to wander around, pick up some locally made crafts, and try some traditional Aboriginal food. The town has a relaxed vibe, and you can often find live music or street performers adding to the atmosphere.

For a more hands-on adventure, you can visit the **Alice Springs Telegraph Station,** a historic site that was once part of the telegraph line connecting Australia to the rest of the world.

The station offers guided tours where you can learn about the history of communication in the region, and it's also a great spot for picnics and walks.

Another exciting activity is **hot air ballooning** over the desert. Alice Springs offers some of the best views of the surrounding landscape from the air. In the early mornings, the skies are filled with colorful hot air balloons floating above the desert, giving you a bird's-eye view of the town, the red sand dunes, and the rugged hills of the Outback.

• **Stargazing in the Outback**

One of the most amazing things about Alice Springs is the night sky. The clear desert air and lack of light pollution make it one of the best places in Australia for stargazing.

The Outback offers a chance to see constellations and stars that you might never have noticed before. You can visit the **Alice Springs Desert Park or Earth Sanctuary** for special night tours where you can learn about the stars and the myths that Aboriginal people associate with the night sky.

The **Astronomical Society of Alice Springs** often holds star parties, where locals and visitors gather to observe the stars through telescopes. The clear skies allow you to see distant galaxies, star clusters, and planets like never before.

• **Best Time to Visit Alice Springs**

The best time for visitation to this place is always from April to October. The weather can get extremely hot in the summer, so visiting in the autumn or spring means more comfortable temperatures for outdoor activities and sightseeing. However, even in the cooler months, it's important to be prepared for chilly evenings and warm days.

There are several places to stay in Alice Springs, from comfortable hotels to more rustic camping options. Many of the accommodations offer tours and packages that allow you to experience the best of

Alice Springs, from camel rides to stargazing tours.

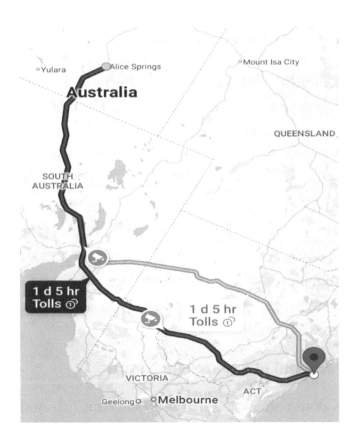

- **The map above shows distance (with time covered) from Sydney to Alice Springs**

Kakadu National Park

Kakadu National Park, located in the Northern Territory of Australia, is one of the most famous natural wonders of the country. It is a place filled with stunning landscapes, diverse wildlife, and a rich cultural history. Kakadu is massive—it spans over 20,000 square kilometers, making it larger than some countries! Whether you're a fan of outdoor adventures, history, or wildlife, Kakadu has something exciting to offer.

• **A Land of Beauty and Nature**

Kakadu is known for its beautiful and diverse landscapes. The park includes everything from tropical wetlands and floodplains to rugged cliffs and ancient rock formations. The land is also home to countless species of animals and plants. Many of these creatures live in the park all year round, while others migrate during different seasons.

The wet season, which runs from November to April, is when the park comes alive with rushing waterfalls and overflowing rivers. During this time, the park is at its greenest, with lush vegetation growing everywhere. **Waterfalls like Jim Jim Falls** and Twin Falls become more impressive, their waters crashing down from high cliffs. These falls are not just beautiful to look at, but they also offer a chance to cool off in the refreshing water during a visit.

In the dry season, from May to October, the landscape changes, and the waterfalls slow down. However, the weather becomes perfect for hiking, wildlife watching, and visiting the ancient rock art sites. No matter when you visit, there's always something special to see in Kakadu.

• **Wildlife in Kakadu**

Kakadu is one of the best places in Australia to see wildlife. The park is home to over 280 species of birds, including the Jabiru, a large black-and-white stork, and the **Rainbow Bee-eater**, a colorful bird known for catching insects mid-flight.

You can also spot crocodiles, which are often seen sunbathing on riverbanks or swimming in the water. There are also plenty of other animals like wallabies, dingoes, wild pigs, and bats that live in Kakadu.

If you enjoy birdwatching, **Yellow Water Billabong** is the perfect place to visit. It's a huge wetland area that's full of life, especially during the wet season when the birds come to nest.

The area can be explored by boat, where you'll float along the waters and see all sorts of wildlife, including saltwater crocodiles and birds like the whistling kite and magpie goose. This is one of the most exciting ways to see wildlife in Kakadu.

For those interested in seeing crocodiles up close, **Cahills Crossing** is a popular spot. This crossing connects the Arnhem Land and Kakadu, and it's known for the large saltwater crocodiles that hang out there, especially during the dry season. But it's important to be cautious, as the crocodiles can be dangerous.

• **Ancient Rock Art**

Kakadu National Park is not only a place of stunning natural beauty, but it's also a place rich in cultural history. The park is home to one of the oldest art galleries in the world, with rock art that's over 20,000 years old. The art was created by the park's Indigenous **Bininj/Mungguy** people, and their ancestors have lived in the area for thousands of years.

One of the best places to see this ancient rock art is at **Ubirr**, where you'll find a collection of paintings on large rock walls. These artworks show animals, people, and scenes from ancient life. Some of the paintings are still very clear and colorful, despite being so old. At Ubirr, you can also climb a rocky outcrop to enjoy a panoramic view of the park and the surrounding wetlands.

Another important site is **Nourlangie Rock.** This is another famous area filled with rock art, and it also has **Aboriginal rock shelters** where people lived thousands of years ago. Nourlangie Rock offers a guided walk where visitors can learn about the significance of the art and the history of the people who created it.

Both of these sites are not only beautiful but also important to the **Aboriginal people** who still live in the region. They have spiritual significance and provide a glimpse into the lives of Australia's first peoples.

• **Waterfalls and Gorges**

Kakadu is also home to some of Australia's most famous waterfalls and gorges. **Jim Jim Falls** is one of the biggest and most impressive waterfalls in Kakadu, with water tumbling over a 200-meter drop. During the wet season, Jim Jim Falls is particularly dramatic, with the water flowing down in full force. It's also a great place to go for a swim in the refreshing waters below the falls, though be aware that it's only accessible during the dry season.

Another beautiful waterfall is **Twin Falls**, which is famous for the way the water splits into two streams as it falls down the cliff. Twin Falls can be reached by a boat cruise followed by a short walk. This area is full of natural beauty, with its peaceful atmosphere and lush vegetation.

If you enjoy hiking and exploring gorges, then **Koolpin Gorge** and **Gunlom Falls** are other great spots to visit. Gunlom Falls has a natural infinity pool at the top, where you can take a swim while enjoying stunning views over the park. Hiking to these spots can be a fun adventure, and the reward of seeing the waterfalls and natural pools makes it all worthwhile.

• **Things to Do in Kakadu**

There's so much to do in Kakadu, no matter what kind of adventure you're looking for. If you enjoy hiking, there are plenty of trails to choose from. For example, the **Mirrai Lookout** walk will give you great views of the wetlands and the surrounding area. If you're interested in cultural experiences, there are several **Aboriginal cultural tours** where you can learn more about the Indigenous people who have lived in the area for thousands of years.

For those who love water, Kakadu offers plenty of opportunities for swimming, boating, and fishing. Whether you're at **Maguk Gorge, Gunlom Falls, or Mardugal Billabong**, you'll find refreshing spots to cool off. But it's important to always be careful when swimming in Kakadu, especially because of the presence of crocodiles in some areas.

Kakadu is also a fantastic place to camp. There are several campgrounds in the park where you can set up a tent or stay in a cabin. Staying overnight in the park gives you the chance to enjoy the natural beauty of Kakadu at sunrise and sunset, when the colors of the sky and the landscape are at their best.

• **Best Time to Visit Kakadu**

The best time for visitation to this place is always from May to October. This is when the weather is cooler, and many of the park's most famous spots, like Jim Jim Falls and Twin Falls, are more accessible. It's also the best time to visit for hiking, camping, and wildlife watching.

If you visit during the wet season (from November to April), keep in mind that some areas of the park may be closed due to flooding. However, the wet season also has its charm, with dramatic waterfalls and lush greenery.

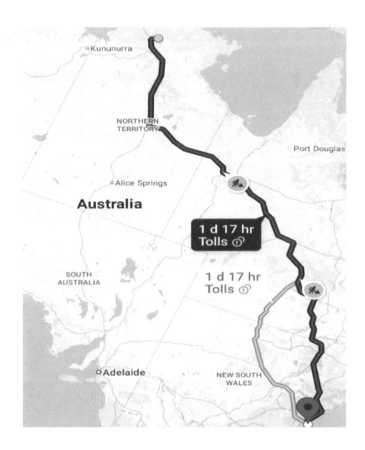

• **The map above shows distance (with time covered) from Sydney to Kakadu National Park**

Darwin

• **The map above shows distance (with time covered) from Sydney central to Darwin**

Darwin is the capital city of the Northern Territory and serves as a gateway to the wonders of the Outback and surrounding regions. It's a unique and vibrant city with a tropical climate, laid-back atmosphere, and a rich history. Whether you're interested in experiencing local markets, learning about WWII history, or having close encounters with some of Australia's most famous wildlife, Darwin has something for everyone. Here's a look at what you can do and see in this exciting city.

• **Mindil Beach Markets**

One of the best ways to experience the local culture in Darwin is by visiting the **Mindil Beach Markets**. These markets are open during the dry season, typically from April to October, and offer a lively and colorful atmosphere. The markets are famous for their food, crafts, and entertainment.

Here, you can find food stalls selling delicious dishes from all over the world, from Asian-inspired curries to Aussie burgers and barbecued seafood. The smell of freshly cooked food fills the air as locals and visitors gather to try something new or enjoy their favorite treat. Whether you want to taste a juicy satay skewer, try a bowl of noodles, or have a sweet treat like a mango ice cream, the Mindil Beach Markets have something for everyone.

Apart from food, the markets are also known for their handmade crafts. You can find jewelry, clothing, artwork, and other souvenirs made by local artists. Many of these items are unique to the Northern Territory, and they make great keepsakes or gifts.

What makes the Mindil Beach Markets even more special is their location. The markets are right by the beach, and visitors can enjoy a stunning view of the sunset over the ocean.

As the sun goes down, the sky turns shades of orange, pink, and purple, creating a beautiful backdrop to the bustling market atmosphere. After exploring the markets, you can relax on the beach and watch the sky change colors as night falls.

• **World War II History in Darwin**

Darwin has an important place in Australia's World War II history, and if you're interested in learning about the past, there are several historic sites and museums to visit.

During the war, Darwin was heavily bombed by the Japanese. In fact, the city was bombed more than 60 times between 1942 and 1943, making it the most bombed city in Australia during the war.

To learn more about this part of history, you can visit the **Darwin Military Museum,** which has an extensive collection of wartime artifacts, photos, and exhibits.

The museum is located at **East Point Reserve**, and it tells the story of how the people of Darwin lived through the bombings and the impact it had on the city. One of the highlights of the museum is its collection of old military vehicles, including tanks, trucks, and artillery used during the war.

Another important site is **The Darwin Cenotaph,** which is a memorial dedicated to all Australians who served in wars. It's located in the heart of the city, and it's a place of reflection for those who want to pay tribute to the soldiers who fought for Australia.

If you're looking for a more hands-on way to learn about WWII history, you can visit the **Tunnels at the Bombing of Darwin** tour. This tour takes you to the underground tunnels used by soldiers during the bombings. The tunnels were built to protect people and supplies from the air raids, and today, visitors can explore these tunnels and learn what life was like for the people who lived through the attacks.

• **Crocodile Encounters**

One of the most famous and exciting things to do in Darwin is to see crocodiles up close. Crocodiles are native to the Northern Territory, and they can be found in rivers, wetlands, and coastal areas throughout the region. Darwin is home to some of the largest saltwater crocodiles in the world, and there are several places where you can have a safe crocodile encounter.

One popular place to visit is the **Crocosaurus Cove** in the city center. This is an interactive reptile park where visitors can see crocodiles of all sizes. One of the most thrilling experiences at Crocosaurus Cove is the **Cage of Death,** where you can enter a clear cage and be lowered into a crocodile's enclosure. Inside the cage, you'll be able to watch the crocodile swim right up to you, and it's an unforgettable experience. Don't worry, though, the cage is strong and safe, so you can enjoy the thrill without any danger.

Another place to visit is the Wildlife Park in the nearby **Litchfield National Park**, where you can see not just crocodiles but also a range of other local animals. The park offers guided tours, and you can learn more about the local wildlife, including wallabies, dingoes, and snakes. If you're lucky, you might even get a chance to feed the crocodiles!

For those looking for a more natural crocodile experience, you can go on a cruise in the nearby **Adelaide River**, known for its large population of saltwater crocodiles. During the cruise, you'll have the chance to see crocodiles in their natural habitat as the boat takes you along the river. The guides often feed the crocodiles to attract them closer to the boat, and you'll get a chance to see them jump out of the water to grab food.

• **Other Things to Do in Darwin**

Aside from the Mindil Beach Markets, WWII history, and crocodile encounters, Darwin offers plenty of other activities for visitors. One of the best places to visit in Darwin is the **Southport Pier,** where you can enjoy a walk along the water, take in views of the harbor, and spot local wildlife. It's also a great place to go for a swim or enjoy a picnic.

Another must-see is **Darwin Harbour**, which is perfect for fishing, boating, or simply relaxing by the water. You can join a harbor cruise to learn about the history of the area or even try your hand at catching a big fish!

If you're interested in Indigenous culture, Darwin has many places that offer a glimpse into the lives of the local Aboriginal people.

The **Museum and Art Gallery of the Northern Territory** is a great place to see Aboriginal art and learn about the history of the region. The gallery often features exhibitions showcasing the culture, traditions, and art of the Northern Territory's Indigenous people.

For those who love nature, Darwin is also home to several beautiful parks and gardens, such as the **Botanic Gardens and Darwin's Lagoon**, where you can enjoy a peaceful day surrounded by tropical plants and wildlife.

• **Best Time to Visit Darwin**

The best time to visit Darwin is during the dry season, which runs from May to October. During this time, the weather is warm but not too hot, and you can enjoy outdoor activities without worrying about heavy rainfall. The dry season is also when the Mindil Beach Markets are open, making it a great time to experience the city's lively atmosphere.

If you don't mind warmer temperatures, you can visit Darwin during the wet season (November to April). This is when the city experiences tropical rains, and the landscape becomes lush and green. Although it can be hot and humid, the wet season has its own charm, with fewer crowds and some beautiful, dramatic thunderstorms.

Exploring the Outback

Known for its rugged landscapes, wide open spaces, and unique wildlife, it's one of the most exciting destinations to visit in Australia. If you're ready for an adventure, taking a road trip through the Outback is a great way to experience this wild and beautiful region. Whether you're driving to the famous Uluru (Ayers Rock), stopping at small desert towns, or spotting animals you won't find anywhere else, the Outback has a lot to offer.

In this guide, we'll look at some of the best road trips you can take, important safety tips, and the must-see places along the way.

• Iconic Road Trips in the Outback

One of the best ways to explore the Outback is by car. It gives you the freedom to stop where you want, take photos of stunning views, and explore hidden spots that you might not see on a tour. Here are a few of the most popular road trips in the Northern Territory:

1. The Red Centre Way

The Red Centre Way is one of the most famous drives in the Outback. Starting in Alice Springs, it takes you on a journey through the heart of the Northern Territory, passing famous landmarks like Uluru and

Kata Tjuta (The Olgas), as well as Kings Canyon.

This 1,100 km loop road trip will show you some of the most iconic landscapes in Australia. Along the way, you'll drive past red deserts, rocky cliffs, and wide-open plains. If you're lucky, you might even spot kangaroos, emus, or camels.

Key stops on the Red Centre Way include:

- **Alice Springs**: This small town is the starting point of the trip. It's a great place to learn about local history and Aboriginal culture.

- **Uluru (Ayers Rock):** The massive red rock formation is one of Australia's most famous landmarks. It's especially stunning at sunrise and sunset when the colors of the rock change dramatically.

- **Kata Tjuta (The Olgas):** A group of giant rock domes, Kata Tjuta is just a short drive from Uluru. It's perfect for a hike through the Valley of the Winds.

- **Kings Canyon:** This beautiful canyon is full of steep cliffs, narrow gorges, and hidden gardens. The **Kings Canyon Rim Walk** offers fantastic views.

2. The Stuart Highway

The **Stuart Highway** runs straight through the middle of Australia, connecting **Adelaide** to Darwin. This highway is perfect for long road trips, and many travelers use it to explore the Outback. The highway is over 2,800 kilometers long, so it takes several days to drive the entire route.

Along the Stuart Highway, you'll pass several interesting stops, including:

- **Coober Pedy**: This small mining town is famous for its underground homes. It's one of the hottest places in Australia, so people live in homes dug into the earth to stay cool.

- **Devils Marbles (Karlu Karlu):** These large, round boulders are scattered across the desert and are a sacred site for local Aboriginal people.

- **Mataranka**: A small town known for its natural hot springs, perfect for relaxing after a long drive.

3. The Oodnadatta Track

If you want to get off the beaten path, the **Oodnadatta Track** is a more rugged road trip.

It runs through the Outback from **Marla** to **William Creek**, passing old railway stations, desert landscapes, and historical sites. It's a great route for those who love history and adventure.

• **Safety Tips for Road Tripping in the Outback**

The Outback is a wild place, and while it's full of natural beauty, it can also be a challenging environment to travel in.

The below are some important safety tips that will help you:

1. Plan Your Route

Before you leave, make sure to plan your route carefully. The Outback is vast, and distances between towns and fuel stations can be huge.

It's important to know where your next stop will be and how far you'll need to drive between fuel stations. Keep a map handy and use GPS to help guide you.

2. Carry Extra Water and Food

In the Outback, temperatures can soar, especially in the summer. Make sure to carry plenty of water and non-perishable food for the journey.

It's recommended to have at least 5 liters of water per person per day, and always have more than you think you'll need. A spare tire and basic car maintenance tools are also important in case of an emergency.

3. Be Thoroughly Informed About Road Conditions And Including Weather

Weather can change quickly in the Outback. Flash floods can happen during the wet season, and roads may become impassable.

So, ensure you always check weather forecasts and condition of roads before setting off.

Also, inform someone back home about your travel plans, especially if you're going to remote areas.

4. Travel During Daylight Hours

Driving at night in the Outback can be dangerous. Animals like kangaroos and camels are more active at night and can be hard to see.

It's best to drive during daylight hours to avoid accidents. If you must drive at night, use your high beams and stay alert.

5. Be Prepared for Remote Areas

Many parts of the Outback are isolated, and mobile phone service is limited. Be sure to carry a satellite phone or an emergency beacon in case you run into trouble. If you're traveling through remote areas, let someone know your exact route and expected arrival time.

• **Must-See Stops in the Outback**

When driving through the Outback, there are plenty of places worth stopping to visit. These are some of the top spots for consideration: **Uluru (Ayers Rock), Kings Canyon, the MacDonnell Ranges, Coober Pedy, and the Devil's Marbles (Karlu Karlu).**

Chapter Five: Melbourne, Tasmania, and Victoria's Coastline

Melbourne

Melbourne is a city that's bursting with life, color, and creativity. As the cultural capital of Australia, it's a place where you can see amazing art, eat delicious food, and explore hidden gems down charming streets.

Whether you're interested in history, shopping, or simply enjoying a good meal, Melbourne has something for everyone. Let's take a look at what makes this vibrant city so special.

• A City of Arts and Culture

One of the first things you'll notice about Melbourne is its love for art and culture.

Everywhere you look, there are murals, galleries, and public art displays that bring the city to life.

This artistic spirit is seen throughout the city in both modern and traditional forms.

• Melbourne's Street Art

Melbourne is famous for its street art. The city has some of the coolest laneways (narrow streets) where artists create large, colorful murals.

The laneways are so important to Melbourne's identity that the city even has a **Street Art Walk** tour, where you can explore some of the best works.

A well-known spot for street art is **AC/DC Lane**, named after the famous rock band.

It's a fun place to walk through and see rock-themed murals that honor the city's music scene.

• The map above shows distance (with time covered) from Sydney central to Melbourne

- **The National Gallery of Victoria (NGV)**

For those who enjoy traditional art, the **National Gallery of Victoria** is a must-visit. It's the oldest and largest public art museum in Australia and is filled with thousands of artworks from all over the world. The NGV's collection includes everything from ancient Egyptian artifacts to modern sculptures. If you're lucky, you may even get to see a special exhibition that features world-famous artists.

- **Melbourne's Famous Laneways and Hidden Gems**

Melbourne's laneways aren't just home to street art; they are also filled with hidden cafes, boutique shops, and interesting places to explore. These narrow, sometimes winding lanes are part of what makes Melbourne so unique.

• **Degraves Street and Centre Place**

If you love food, **Degraves Street** is the perfect place to visit. It's known for its outdoor cafes and delicious coffee. The street is always buzzing with people, from locals enjoying their morning brew to tourists trying to find the best croissant.

Just a short walk from Degraves is **Centre Place,** another laneway where you can find more cafes, quirky shops, and street art. These are great places to just sit back and soak in the atmosphere of Melbourne.

• **Block Arcade and Royal Arcade**

For a more classic experience, visit **Block Arcade and Royal Arcade,** which are historic shopping arcades in the heart of the city.

Both arcades have a Victorian-style charm, with old-school shops selling everything from jewelry to handmade chocolates.

At the Royal Arcade, you can also see the **Gaunt's Clock,** which has been ringing the hours since 1891.

• **Dining in Melbourne**

Melbourne is also known for its food scene. People from all over the world have brought their unique flavors to the city, making it a food lover's paradise.

Whether you're craving Italian pasta, Asian street food, or a classic Aussie pie, you'll find it in Melbourne.

• **Queen Victoria Market**

One of the best places to taste Melbourne's food culture is **Queen Victoria Market.** It's one of the largest open-air markets in the Southern Hemisphere and is filled with fresh produce, cheeses, meats, and prepared foods.

It's the perfect spot to grab a quick bite or buy ingredients to cook your own meals.

The market is also home to food stalls offering street food from around the world, including Turkish gozleme, Indonesian satay, and Italian pizza.

• **Chinatown Melbourne**

Melbourne's **Chinatown** is another great place to eat. Located in the heart of the city, it's filled with authentic Asian restaurants that serve everything from dim sum to noodle soups. Some of the best Chinese restaurants in Melbourne are tucked away in alleys off Little Bourke Street. A popular dish here is **Peking duck**, which is crispy and served with pancakes and hoisin sauce.

• **Lygon Street**

If you love Italian food, **Lygon Street** in the Carlton neighborhood is the place to be. Known as Melbourne's "Little Italy," this street is lined with family-owned restaurants serving pizza, pasta, and gelato. The lively atmosphere makes it a fun place to enjoy a meal with friends or family. You can also explore nearby cafes that make excellent coffee, a Melburnian favorite.

• Melbourne's Coffee Culture

Melbourne is one of the world's best cities for coffee lovers. The city has a long history of coffee culture, and it's said that Melbourne's baristas (people who make coffee) are among the best in the world. If you're a fan of coffee, you'll want to check out some of Melbourne's most famous coffee spots.

• Specialty Coffee Shops

In neighborhoods like **Fitzroy and Collingwood,** you'll find trendy cafes that take their coffee seriously. These cafes often serve single-origin coffee, where the beans are sourced from specific farms or regions, and prepared in a variety of ways like pour-over, espresso, or cold brew. **Proud Mary and St. Ali** are two of the most popular coffee spots, known for their strong brews and relaxed vibes.

• Melbourne's Laneway Cafes

As you wander around the laneways of Melbourne, you'll also come across hidden cafes tucked in corners or behind alley doors. These places often serve specialty coffee and homemade pastries. They're great for when you need a break from sightseeing and want to enjoy a quiet cup of coffee.

• Melbourne's Iconic Buildings and Landmarks

Beyond the food and street art, Melbourne also has some impressive buildings and landmarks that are worth visiting.

• Flinders Street Station

One of Melbourne's most recognizable landmarks is **Flinders Street Station**. It's a beautiful yellow-and-cream building with a large clock on the front, right in the center of the city. It's the main railway station, but it's also a popular spot for tourists. You can often see people taking photos in front of the station or sitting in the nearby gardens.

• **Royal Botanic Gardens**

If you love nature, don't miss the **Royal Botanic Gardens**. Located near the center of Melbourne, the gardens are a peaceful retreat with over 8,500 plant species from around the world. You can walk around the large lakes, spot local wildlife like ducks and swans, or even take a guided tour to learn more about the plants.

• **Eureka Skydeck**

For an amazing view of Melbourne, visit the **Eureka Skydeck** in the **Eureka Tower**. Located on the 88th floor, it's the highest observation deck in the Southern Hemisphere. From here, you can see the entire city and beyond, all the way to the bay. On clear days, the view is incredible, and it's a perfect spot to take photos.

The Great Ocean Road

The Great Ocean Road is one of the most famous and beautiful coastal drives in the world. Stretching over 240 kilometers along the south coast of Victoria, Australia, this road offers breathtaking views, interesting landmarks, and a chance to experience nature in its most stunning form.

Whether you love the sea, surfing, or just want to enjoy a drive, the Great Ocean Road has something for everyone.

• A Scenic Drive Along the Coast

The Great Ocean Road is known for its winding paths along cliffs that overlook the ocean, making every turn feel like an adventure.

As you drive, you'll be treated to incredible views of the Southern Ocean and its rugged coastline. The road itself is a journey filled with surprises—every few kilometers, you can pull over to admire a new view or explore a hidden gem.

One of the highlights of this drive is the chance to see **the famous Twelve Apostles,** a series of tall limestone stacks rising out of the ocean.

These natural formations were created by thousands of years of erosion, and they stand tall and proud against the waves. The Twelve Apostles are one of the most photographed spots along the Great Ocean Road, especially at sunrise or sunset when the light makes the rocks look golden.

Along the way, you'll also pass through towns like **Apollo Bay** and **Port Campbell**, where you can stop for a meal or to stretch your legs. These charming towns have beaches, parks, and little shops that make the journey even more enjoyable.

• **The Twelve Apostles**

The Twelve Apostles are the most famous landmark on the Great Ocean Road. They are located near **Port Campbell National Park**, where you'll find a viewing platform that lets you see these magnificent rock formations up close. The Twelve Apostles were once part of a larger coastline, but over time, the harsh waves and winds caused parts of the cliffs to collapse, leaving behind the giant rock stacks you see today.

Despite their name, there are actually only eight Apostles left, as some of the formations have fallen into the sea. However, the remaining stacks are still an incredible sight. The rocks stand about 45 meters high, and they rise dramatically from the water. The surrounding coastline is equally impressive, with cliffs that stretch out to the horizon, creating a perfect backdrop for photos.The waters around the Twelve Apostles are home to dolphins, seals, and sometimes even whales during their migration periods.

• Surfing Along the Coast

For those who enjoy surfing, the Great Ocean Road offers some of the best surf spots in Australia. The area is known for its strong waves and surf-friendly beaches, making it a popular destination for surfers from around the world.

• Bells Beach

One of the most famous surfing locations along the Great Ocean Road is **Bells Beach**, located near **Torquay.** Bells Beach is famous for hosting the **Rip Curl Pro,** one of the most important surfing competitions in the world. The beach itself has long, powerful waves that attract both professional surfers and beginners looking to test their skills.

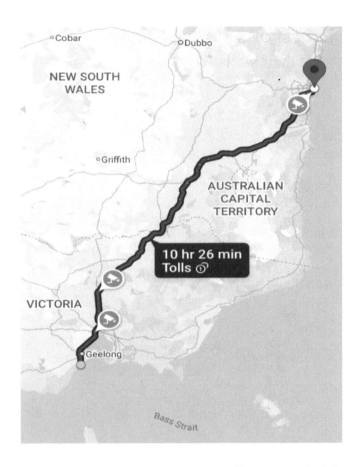

• **The map above shows distance (with time covered) from Sydney central to Bells Beach**

Even if you're not a surfer, watching the surfers catch waves at Bells Beach can be a thrilling experience.

The waves here can reach up to 6 meters, and the view from the cliffs above the beach is stunning, especially at sunset when the sky lights up in bright oranges and reds.

• **Lorne and Apollo Bay**

If you're a beginner or looking for a quieter spot to surf, **Lorne and Apollo Bay** offer more relaxed beaches with smaller waves.

These towns are perfect for families or anyone looking to try surfing for the first time. The beaches here are clean, with golden sand and clear water. Local surf schools offer lessons for beginners, so even if you've never surfed before, you can give it a go.

• Rainforests, Waterfalls, and Wildlife

Beyond the ocean, the Great Ocean Road also takes you through lush rainforests and past stunning waterfalls. The **Great Otway National Park** is a highlight of the drive, with towering trees, beautiful walking trails, and hidden waterfalls like **Triplet Falls and Beauchamp Falls.** The forest feels magical, with moss-covered trees and birds singing overhead. If you're lucky, you might even see koalas and kangaroos along the way.

Maits Rest is a popular stop in the Otway Ranges. This area has a short walking track that takes you through a cool, shaded rainforest. The path is surrounded by ferns, tall trees, and streams, making it a peaceful place to relax and enjoy nature.

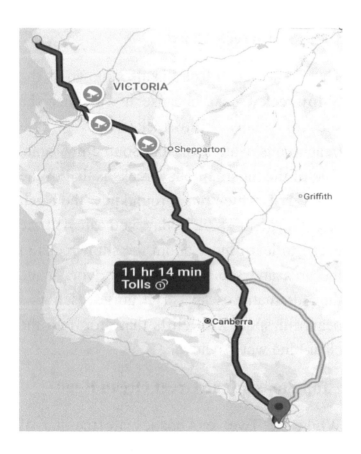

• The map above shows distance (with time covered) from Sydney to The Great Ocean Road

• **The Shipwreck Coast**

The Great Ocean Road is also known as the **Shipwreck Coast** because it was once the site of many shipwrecks due to the treacherous waters of the Southern Ocean. One of the most famous wrecks is that of the **Loch Ard**, which ran aground near the **Loch Ard Gorge** in 1878. Today, you can visit the gorge to learn more about the shipwrecks in the area and see where the survivors made their dramatic escape. The gorge itself is a beautiful spot, with cliffs that drop into the clear blue water below.

• **Top Stops on the Great Ocean Road**

While the Twelve Apostles are the star of the show, there are plenty of other great stops along the Great Ocean Road that make the trip even more special.

1. Torquay

Known as the birthplace of Australian surfing, Torquay is a lively town where you can learn about surfing history or shop for surf gear. It's also home to great beaches for swimming and surfing.

2. Anglesea

This small town is perfect for a relaxing stop. It's surrounded by nature, with walking trails that lead through the bush and along the coast.

3. Warrnambool

This town is known for its whale watching. If you visit between June and September, you might see Southern Right Whales migrating along the coast.

4. Cape Otway

Visit the **Cape Otway Lighthouse**, which has been guiding ships safely along the coast since 1848. The lighthouse is one of the oldest in Australia and offers amazing views of the coastline.

5. Port Fairy

A charming town that feels like it's frozen in time, Port Fairy is a great place to walk around and enjoy some of the best-preserved historical buildings on the coast.

Phillip Island

Phillip Island is a special place just off the coast of Melbourne, Victoria. It's famous for its beautiful landscapes, friendly wildlife, and, of course, the incredible Penguin Parade. Whether you're looking to see amazing animals, enjoy a day at the beach, or learn about the local nature, Phillip Island offers a perfect mix of fun activities for the whole family.

• The Penguin Parade

The highlight of any visit to Phillip Island is the **Penguin Parade.** Every night, as the sun sets, little **Fairy Penguins** make their way from the ocean back to their burrows on the island. These penguins, the smallest species of penguins in the world, waddle across the sand in large groups. It's a magical sight to see them come ashore after spending the day fishing in the cold waters of Bass Strait.

At the **Phillip Island Nature Park,** there is a viewing area where visitors can watch the penguins in a way that doesn't disturb them. The penguins' journey is quite a spectacle: they carefully march up the beach, flapping their flippers and chirping to each other as they make their way to their burrows in the sand dunes. The Penguin Parade is especially fun for kids because the penguins are so small and cute!

If you want a closer look, there are special **Penguin Plus or Underground Viewing** options, where you can see the penguins even more up close, without interrupting their natural behaviors.

• **Wildlife Encounters**

Phillip Island is not just about penguins—it's also a great place to see other Australian wildlife in their natural habitats.

• **Koala Conservation Centre**

One of the best places to see koalas is the **Koala Conservation Centre.** This center is set within a peaceful forest where koalas live in the wild, so you won't just see them in cages or enclosures. Here, you can walk along elevated boardwalks that take you through the trees, where koalas can be seen lounging and napping in the branches. The koalas are often so relaxed that you can get a good look at them without disturbing them.

Koalas sleep for up to 18 hours a day, so there's a good chance you'll see one snoozing in the trees. It's an awesome place for kids to learn about these adorable creatures and understand why they need help to stay safe in the wild.

• **Phillip Island Wildlife Park**

If you want to see even more animals, the **Phillip Island Wildlife Park** is another fantastic stop. Here, you can get up close to kangaroos, wallabies, emus, and many other native animals. You can even hand-feed kangaroos, which is an exciting experience for kids. The park also has a variety of birds and reptiles, giving you a chance to see animals from all over Australia.

If you visit at the right time, you might also spot some native Australian birds like kookaburras and lorikeets, or even a few wild animals passing through the park.

• Local Beaches

Aside from the wildlife, Phillip Island has plenty of beautiful beaches where you can relax and enjoy the sun. Whether you want to swim, surf, or simply enjoy the view, the island offers a variety of beaches that are perfect for a family day out.

• Summerland Beach

Summerland Beach is the place to go if you want to see the Penguin Parade up close. It's the beach where the penguins come ashore every evening.

During the day, it's a great spot to relax and enjoy the sand and surf. The beach has soft golden sand and clear blue water, making it a perfect spot for a swim or a picnic. Keep an eye out for wildlife as well, as this area is often visited by seals and dolphins.

• **Cape Woolamai**

If you love surfing or simply enjoy watching surfers, **Cape Woolamai** is one of the best beaches on Phillip Island. It's known for its powerful waves, making it a popular destination for experienced surfers.

Even if you're not into surfing, the beach is beautiful and offers a great place to walk, with stunning views of the coastline.

The nearby **Cape Woolamai State Nature Reserve** is also home to many seabirds, so it's a great spot for birdwatching.

• **Cowes Beach**

For a calmer beach experience, **Cowes Beach** is a great option. Located near the main town of Cowes, this beach is perfect for families with small kids. The water is usually calm, and the shallow areas make it safe for swimming. The beach also has picnic areas and playgrounds, so it's an ideal spot for a family day by the sea. Cowes is also the place to find local shops, cafes, and restaurants if you're looking for a bite to eat after a day at the beach.

• **Nobbies Centre and Seal Rocks**

For an unforgettable nature experience, head to the **Nobbies Centre,** which is located on the western tip of Phillip Island.

From here, you can enjoy panoramic views of the coast and spot the famous **Seal Rocks,** home to one of the largest fur seal colonies in Australia.

While you can't visit the rocks up close, you can watch the seals from the boardwalk, which has telescopes set up to help you get a better view.

The **Nobbies Centre** also offers an educational exhibit about the local marine life, including the seals and the surrounding environment. It's a great spot to learn about the wildlife and the importance of protecting these animals and their habitats.

• Phillip Island Grand Prix Circuit

If you're a fan of cars or motorsports, you might want to check out the **Phillip Island Grand Prix Circuit.** This world-class race track is home to the **Australian Motorcycle Grand Prix** and other exciting events throughout the year. Even if you're not visiting during a race, you can still visit the circuit and take a guided tour to learn about the history of the track. Kids will enjoy seeing the fast cars and bikes and may even get a chance to try a go-kart race!

• **The map above shows distance (with time covered) from Sydney central to Phillip Island**

Tasmania

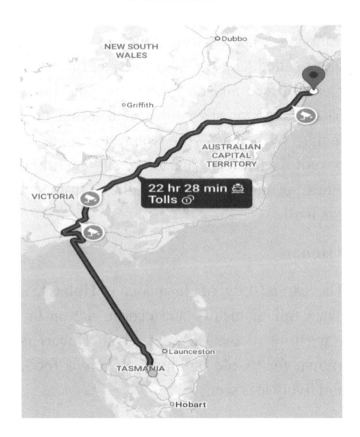

• The map above shows distance (with time covered) from Sydney to Tasmania

Tasmania, Australia's island state, is a place filled with stunning landscapes, amazing wildlife, and delicious food. It's often called "Tassie" by locals, and it offers plenty to see and do for anyone who loves nature, outdoor adventures, and trying new things. Whether you want to hike in beautiful national parks, visit charming cities, or taste local specialties, Tasmania has it all.

• **Hobart**

The capital city of Tasmania is **Hobart,** a place full of history and charm. Set on the waterfront of the Derwent River, Hobart is known for its old buildings, delicious food, and lively arts scene.

One of the best places to visit in Hobart is **Salamanca Place**, a historic area full of sandstone buildings. On Saturdays, the **Salamanca Market** comes alive with local stalls selling everything from fresh food to handmade crafts. It's a great spot to try some Tasmanian cheese, fresh produce, or even a tasty pie.

Another famous spot in Hobart is **MONA, the Museum of Old and New Art.** This modern museum is unlike any other, with quirky exhibits and artwork that will make you think. You can take a ferry from Hobart's waterfront to reach the museum, which is set on the beautiful Moorilla Estate, overlooking the river.

If you enjoy nature and want a great view of the city, take a trip up to **Mount Wellington**. This mountain stands tall over Hobart, and on a clear day, you can see all the way across the city to the water and beyond. You can either drive or hike to the top, and once you're there, the views are amazing.

• **Cradle Mountain**

If you love hiking and want to experience Tasmania's wild beauty, **Cradle Mountain** is a must-see. This national park is home to some of the most famous hiking trails in the world. The mountain itself is a stunning sight with its jagged peaks and lush forests.

The **Overland Track** is a popular multi-day hike that takes you through forests, lakes, and mountains. While it's a tough trail, it's also one of the best ways to see Tasmania's wilderness up close. If you don't want to hike for days, you can still enjoy shorter walks around the **Cradle Mountain-Lake St Clair National Park**. The **Dove Lake Circuit** is an easy, family-friendly trail that offers incredible views of the mountain and the surrounding area.

At Cradle Mountain, you can also spot some of Tasmania's unique wildlife, like **Tasmanian devils, wombats, and wallabies.** There's even a chance to see the rare **pademelon,** a small kangaroo-like animal. The park is a perfect place to get out and enjoy the fresh air while surrounded by stunning scenery.

• **Freycinet National Park**

For a mix of mountains, beaches, and wildlife, **Freycinet National Park** is another one of Tasmania's gems. Located on the east coast, this park is famous for its white sandy beaches, crystal-clear waters, and pink granite mountains. The best-known spot in Freycinet is **Wineglass Bay**, a beach with soft sand and water that looks like it's straight out of a postcard.

You can get to Wineglass Bay by walking the **Wineglass Bay Lookout** trail. The hike is about 1.5 to 2 hours round trip, and the view from the top is absolutely breathtaking. If you're up for a longer adventure, you can continue down to the beach itself and enjoy the sand and water.

Freycinet is also home to other great beaches, like **Hazards Beach,** which is perfect for a peaceful day by the sea. If you're into wildlife, keep an eye out for seals, dolphins, and even whales if you visit during the right season. There are also plenty of spots for kayaking, making it a fun place for families who want to enjoy the outdoors.

• **Local Food**

One of the best things about Tasmania is the food. The island's cool climate and fertile land make it perfect for growing fresh produce, and the local food is some of the best in Australia.

A visit to **Hobart's Salamanca Market** is a great way to taste local treats, but there are other places to try Tasmania's food too. The **Tasmanian Salmon** is world-famous, and you can find it at many restaurants and markets. Tasmanian cheese, like **King Island Dairy** cheese, is also a must-try. If you love chocolate, don't miss out on **Rococo Chocolates** in Hobart, which makes delicious handcrafted chocolates.

In addition to seafood, Tasmania is known for its fresh apples, berries, and honey. You'll find plenty of places to sample these at local farms or markets. **Bruny Island** is another place where you can try amazing local food, including fresh oysters and cheese. It's a small island just off the coast of Tasmania, and it's easy to take a day trip to visit.

• **Other Things to Do in Tasmania**

While Hobart, Cradle Mountain, and Freycinet are the most popular spots, there's plenty more to do in Tasmania. For example, **Port Arthur** is a historic site where you can learn about the island's past as a former convict settlement. The **Tasman Peninsula** is full of rugged cliffs and coastal views, making it a great place for photography.

If you're interested in animals, **Bonorong Wildlife Sanctuary** is a place where you can meet some of Tasmania's most famous animals, including the **Tasmanian devil**. It's a great place to learn about these creatures and how they are being protected.

Tasmania also has a cool climate, which makes it perfect for visiting at any time of the year. During the summer, you can enjoy hiking and beach trips, while in the winter, you can warm up with a cozy meal in one of the island's many great restaurants.

Chapter Six: Perth, Western Australia, and South Australian Wonders

Perth

Perth, the capital city of Western Australia, is a vibrant and exciting place where you can enjoy a mix of beautiful nature, fun outdoor activities, and modern urban attractions.

The city is known for its sunshine, stunning beaches, and the peaceful Swan River that flows through it.

Perth offers something for everyone, whether you love nature, history, or simply relaxing by the water. Let's take a closer look at what makes Perth such a great place to visit.

• **Swan River**

The **Swan River** is one of Perth's most famous features. This long, winding river stretches across the city, offering plenty of places to enjoy the view or take part in outdoor activities. Many people love walking, cycling, or jogging along the riverbanks, enjoying the peaceful surroundings and watching the boats sail by.

You can take a ferry ride along the Swan River, which is a great way to see the city from the water. The ferry ride is not only relaxing but also gives you a chance to spot wildlife, like swans, ducks, and sometimes even dolphins. Another popular activity on the river is kayaking. If you're feeling adventurous, you can rent a kayak and paddle down the river while enjoying the fresh air and stunning views of the city skyline and parks.

The Swan River also has many parks and green spaces along its edge. If you want to spend a day enjoying nature, you can pack a picnic and relax at one of the river's parks, such as **Elizabeth Quay**, which has beautiful walkways, playgrounds, and places to eat. This area is perfect for families, with plenty of open space to enjoy a sunny day.

• **Beaches**

Perth is famous for its beautiful beaches, and it's no wonder why! The city is located on the coast, meaning you have easy access to some of the best beaches in Australia. Whether you like to swim, surf, or simply relax on the sand, there's a beach for you in Perth.

Cottesloe Beach is one of the most popular beaches in the city. Known for its soft white sand and crystal-clear water, it's a great spot for swimming, snorkeling, and watching the sunset. The beach has cafes and restaurants nearby, so after a swim, you can grab a bite to eat while enjoying the ocean view.

Another great beach in Perth is **Scarborough Beach**. This beach is perfect for families and surfers alike. With its large waves, Scarborough is known for being a great surfing spot. If you're not into surfing, you can just relax on the beach or take a walk along the coast to enjoy the view.

For those who like to explore quieter, more peaceful beaches, **Trigg Beach** is a great option. It's a little less crowded, making it perfect for a more relaxing day by the water. Many people also like to walk along the coastal paths that lead to hidden beaches, making it a fun way to spend time outdoors.

• **Kings Park**

One of Perth's best features is Kings Park, a huge park right in the middle of the city. It's one of the largest inner-city parks in the world, offering lots of space to walk, relax, and take in the views. From Kings Park, you can see the entire city, including the Swan River and Perth's skyline. It's a great place for a family picnic, a casual stroll, or to just sit and enjoy the scenery.

There are many walking trails throughout the park, and some paths lead to **the State War Memorial**, which is a beautiful spot to learn about Australia's history. If you love nature, you can visit the **Botanic Garden** within Kings Park, which features thousands of native Australian plants. It's an amazing place to learn about the country's unique plants and wildlife.

For something really special, visit Kings Park at sunset. The views of the city and river are incredible, especially when the sun sets over the water, turning everything a golden color. It's the perfect place to take photos or just relax and enjoy the natural beauty of Perth.

• **Urban Attractions**

Perth has plenty of fun things to do if you want to enjoy the city's modern attractions. The city is home to many museums, art galleries, and shopping areas, making it a great place to spend a day learning or shopping.

The Perth Cultural Centre is one of the main places to go if you love art and history. The **Art Gallery of Western Australia** has a huge collection of Australian art, while the **Western Australian Museum** is perfect for those interested in natural history. The museum has exhibits on dinosaurs, the state's wildlife, and even the history of the Aboriginal people in Western Australia.

For something a little different, check out **Elizabeth Quay**, a waterfront area that has shops, restaurants, and entertainment. This area is great for families, with playgrounds and spaces for people to enjoy outdoor events. You can also take a walk along the boardwalk and enjoy the views of the Swan River.

If you like animals, the **Perth Zoo** is a great place to visit. Located in South Perth, the zoo is home to many animals, including kangaroos, koalas, and Australian native species. It's a fun and educational experience for kids and families alike.

• **Local Food and Dining**

Perth is a fantastic place to try delicious food. With its mix of cultures and coastal location, you can find a wide variety of dishes from different parts of the world. Whether you like seafood, international cuisine, or local Australian food, there's something for every taste.

If you love seafood, Perth's location on the coast means you can find fresh fish, prawns, and oysters in many restaurants. Try some fish and chips by the beach for a classic

Aussie meal, or head to one of the city's high-end restaurants for a more refined experience.

Perth is also known for its **local wine**. Western Australia's **Margaret River** region, not far from Perth, is famous for producing some of the best wines in the country. Many restaurants in Perth serve locally made wines, and you can visit wineries in the nearby countryside to taste some for yourself.

If you're in the mood for something sweet, don't forget to try **Tim Tams,** a popular Australian chocolate biscuit, or enjoy a traditional **Aussie pie** at one of the local bakeries. These snacks are loved by locals and visitors alike.

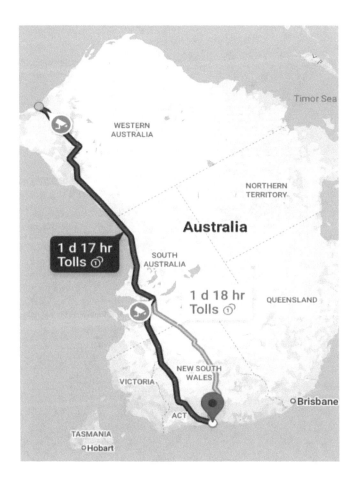

- The map above shows distance (with time covered) from Sydney central to Perth

Margaret River

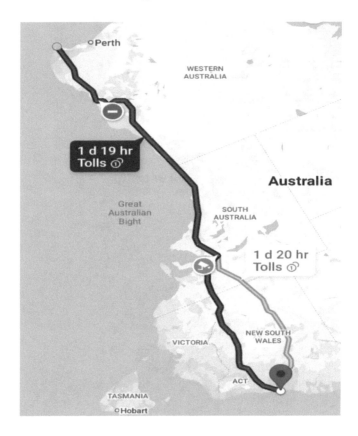

• The map above shows distance (with time covered) from Sydney to Margaret River

Located in the southwest of Western Australia, **Margaret River is a beautiful place known for its stunning beaches, amazing food, world-class wine, and laid-back surf culture.** If you love nature, great food, or surfing, Margaret River is the place to be. Whether you're visiting for a weekend or a longer trip, this small town offers plenty to do for everyone. Let's take a closer look at what makes Margaret River such a special spot.

• **A Taste of Wine**

One of the main reasons people visit Margaret River is because it's famous for its wine. The area has some of the best vineyards in Australia, producing high-quality wines that are loved by people all around the world. The **Margaret River Wine Region** is home to over 200 wineries, many of which offer wine tasting experiences for visitors.

If you visit, you'll have the chance to try some amazing local wines, like **Chardonnay and Cabernet Sauvignon,** which are grown in the region's perfect climate. Many wineries have beautiful outdoor areas where you can sit, enjoy a glass of wine, and take in the views of the rolling vineyards. Some popular wineries in the area include **Leeuwin Estate and Vasse Felix,** both of which are well-known for their delicious wines and great food.

The vineyards aren't just about wine—they often host events, live music, and festivals. You can even join a tour to learn more about how the wine is made, from growing the grapes to the final bottle. If you're interested in learning about wine, this is the perfect place.

• **Gourmet Food**

Along with wine, Margaret River is also known for its fantastic food. The region offers a wide variety of fresh produce, seafood, and gourmet treats that make it a food lover's dream.

Seafood lovers will be happy to know that Margaret River is famous for its fresh fish, prawns, and oysters. You can try these at local restaurants or buy them straight from the source at the **Margaret River Farmers Market.** The market is held on weekends and is the best place to find fresh, local produce, cheeses, and baked goods.

For those who enjoy a meal with a view, many of the restaurants in the area offer outdoor seating where you can look out over vineyards, forests, or the ocean while enjoying a delicious meal. One of the best-known restaurants is **Miki's Open Kitchen,** a place where you can enjoy fresh, local dishes made from the finest ingredients.

Margaret River also has a number of cafes and bakeries where you can stop for coffee, cakes, and pastries. You can even enjoy local specialties like chocolate made with ingredients from the region. The variety of food in Margaret River is impressive, so there's always something new to try, whether you're dining in a fancy restaurant or having a quick snack at a local cafe.

• Surf Culture

If you love the beach and surfing, Margaret River is the perfect place for you. The town is surrounded by some of the best beaches in Australia, and it's known for its strong surf culture. Margaret River is famous for its consistent waves, making it a top destination for surfers from all over the world.

Prevelly Beach, located just outside of town, is one of the most famous surfing spots in the area. It's known for its powerful waves, which attract both beginners and professional surfers. The beach is a beautiful spot to relax as well, with golden sand and clear water perfect for swimming or just lounging in the sun.

For those who want to learn how to surf, there are plenty of surf schools in the area. Whether you're a first-time surfer or looking to improve your skills, instructors are available to guide you through the process. Surfing isn't the only water activity in Margaret River—kayaking, paddleboarding, and snorkeling are also popular options.

Besides the surf, Margaret River's beaches are great for relaxing, walking, and watching the sunset. Many of the beaches offer stunning views, with tall cliffs and clear water that create a perfect backdrop for a peaceful day by the ocean.

• **Nature and Adventure**

Aside from its food, wine, and surf, Margaret River is surrounded by beautiful nature. The region is full of forests, caves, and rivers, making it a great place for outdoor activities.

The **Lceuwin-Naturaliste National Park** is one of the best places to visit if you love hiking and exploring nature. The park has many walking trails that take you through tall forests, past waterfalls, and along the coast. The **Cape to Cape Track** is a popular hiking trail that stretches along the coastline for 135 kilometers, offering incredible views of the ocean and forests. Along the way, you'll find unique wildlife and plants, making it a great place for nature lovers.

Margaret River is also home to some interesting caves, like the **Lake Cave and Jewel Cave**. These caves are known for their beautiful limestone formations, and guided tours are available to help you learn about the cave's history and geology. Exploring these caves is a fun way to discover more about the natural wonders of the area.

If you prefer something a little more laid-back, there are plenty of parks, nature reserves, and quiet beaches to visit. **Boranup Forest**, with its tall Karri trees, is a peaceful place to walk and enjoy the fresh air. There are also plenty of places to go cycling or birdwatching if you're interested in nature.

• **Cultural Experiences**

Margaret River is not just about wine and beaches—it also has a rich cultural history. The region is home to the **Noongar** people, the traditional owners of the land. If you want to learn more about their culture, you can visit the **Boodjidup Nature Reserve**, which is an important site for the Noongar people. There are also cultural tours available that can teach you about the traditions and stories of the indigenous people.

You can also learn about the history of the area at the **Margaret River Historical Society Museum,** which showcases the town's past. The museum tells the story of the local settlers, the timber industry, and the development of the area into the vibrant town it is today.

Ningaloo Reef

Located off the coast of Western Australia, **Ningaloo Reef** is one of the most special places in the world for anyone who loves the ocean. This amazing reef stretches over 260 kilometers along the coast and is one of the largest coral reefs in the world. What makes Ningaloo Reef unique is that it is easily accessible from the shore, unlike other famous reefs that require long boat rides. This means you can enjoy the beauty of the reef right from the beach!

Ningaloo Reef is a UNESCO World Heritage site, known for its crystal-clear waters, colorful coral gardens, and rich marine life. But the main reason many people visit the reef is to have the incredible experience of swimming with whale sharks. These gentle giants, the largest fish in the world, visit Ningaloo Reef every year, making it one of the best places on Earth to have this amazing encounter. Let's take a closer look at what makes Ningaloo Reef such a special destination.

• **Whale Shark Experiences**

The whale shark is the star of Ningaloo Reef. These huge fish can grow as long as a bus, but they are completely harmless to humans. Swimming alongside them is a once-in-a-lifetime experience that people travel from all over the world to enjoy. The best time to see whale sharks in Ningaloo is between March and August, when they come to the reef to feed on plankton, the tiny creatures that float in the water.

Tours are available that take you out on boats to see the whale sharks up close. These tours are led by experienced guides who know how to keep both the swimmers and the whale sharks safe. It's important to remember that you don't touch the whale sharks—they are wild animals. But seeing one up close, gliding gracefully through the water, is truly magical. You'll be able to snorkel just a few meters away, observing these amazing creatures in their natural environment.

While whale sharks are the main draw, Ningaloo Reef is also home to many other incredible marine animals. You can spot manta rays, turtles, and even dolphins during your visit. Some lucky visitors may even see humpback whales during their migration. This makes Ningaloo Reef one of the best places in the world for marine wildlife enthusiasts.

• **Pristine Reefs**

Even if you don't want to swim with whale sharks, Ningaloo Reef offers plenty of other opportunities to explore the underwater world. The reef is full of vibrant coral gardens, home to thousands of colorful fish and marine creatures. Whether you prefer snorkeling or scuba diving, you can get up close to the reef's beauty without having to travel far from the shore.

Turquoise Bay is one of the most popular spots for snorkeling. Located in **Cape Range National Park,** this beach is famous for its clear water and the incredible marine life you can see just by swimming a short distance from the shore. It's a great place to see schools of tropical fish, coral, and even sea turtles. The warm, clear waters make it easy to see everything, and the reef is right there, just waiting for you to explore.

If you're into scuba diving, Ningaloo Reef has some fantastic dive spots. The **Mettam's Pool and The Muiron Islands** are known for their great visibility and healthy coral reefs. Scuba divers can explore deeper parts of the reef, where they can see not only vibrant coral but also large schools of fish, reef sharks, and even the occasional dugong, a sea creature that looks like a mix between a manatee and a dolphin.

• **Other Marine Life at Ningaloo Reef**

While whale sharks are the main attraction, the reef is home to many other incredible animals. **Manta rays** are commonly spotted here, especially around the Muiron Islands. These gentle creatures have huge, flat bodies with wings that span up to 7 meters. You can sometimes see them gliding gracefully through the water near the reef.

Sea turtles are another highlight of Ningaloo Reef. Several species of sea turtles, like the green sea turtle and the hawksbill turtle, call the reef home. Some come here to lay their eggs on the sandy beaches. You might even be lucky enough to witness the hatchlings making their way into the sea—a rare and beautiful sight.

If you enjoy spotting dolphins, Ningaloo Reef is a great place to see them too. Dolphins can often be spotted playing near the shore or swimming alongside boats. The reef is also home to a variety of colorful fish, such as parrotfish, clownfish, and wrasse. The waters here are alive with activity, making it a fantastic place for anyone interested in marine life.

• The Coral Gardens

One of the highlights of Ningaloo Reef is its stunning coral gardens. These underwater landscapes are full of colorful corals, sea fans, and sponges that provide a home for hundreds of species of fish and other creatures. The reef is incredibly healthy, thanks to its protected status, and it's one of the best places in the world to see coral reefs in their natural, undisturbed state.

The **Lesser Nannygai** area is famous for its healthy coral formations and is a great spot for both snorkeling and diving. Here, you can see large soft corals, brain corals, and staghorn corals in bright colors. The diversity of coral species is incredible, and it's easy to see why Ningaloo Reef is considered one of the world's best-preserved coral reefs.

• **Getting to Ningaloo Reef**

Ningaloo Reef is located about 1,200 kilometers north of Perth, making it a bit of a journey to reach. The closest town to the reef is **Exmouth,** which has a small airport with flights from Perth. From there, you can hire a car and explore the surrounding areas, including the reef and the nearby **Cape Range National Park.**

If you're looking for a more affordable option, there are also buses that run from Perth to Exmouth, though it takes much longer. Once you arrive in Exmouth, the reef is easy to reach by car, and there are plenty of accommodations in the area, from campsites to luxury resorts.

• **Best Time to Visit Ningaloo Reef**

The best time to visit Ningaloo Reef is during the **whale shark season** from March to August, but the reef is beautiful all year round. If you're interested in snorkeling or diving, any time between April and November is ideal. The water temperature is warm, and the visibility is usually excellent.

However, if you want to witness the **humpback whale migration,** the best time to visit is from September to November, when the whales pass through the area on their way south.

Adelaide and Surrounds

Adelaide, the capital of South Australia, is a lively city surrounded by beautiful countryside, famous vineyards, and stunning coastal spots. It's a place where you can enjoy both the calm of nature and the excitement of city life. The area around Adelaide offers so much to see and do, whether you're a food lover, a history buff, or someone who enjoys outdoor adventures.

• The Barossa Valley

One of the biggest attractions near Adelaide is the **Barossa Valley**, a world-renowned wine region just an hour's drive from the city. The valley is famous for its vineyards, producing some of the best wines in Australia. When you visit, you'll find yourself surrounded by rolling hills covered in rows of grapevines, perfect for a scenic day trip.

The Barossa is home to a variety of wineries, many of which offer guided tours, wine tastings, and delicious meals. **Jacob's Creek** is one of the most famous wineries here. Visitors can tour the winery, taste different wines, and learn about how the wine is made. If you're not old enough to drink, you can still enjoy the beauty of the vineyards and the fun activities the wineries offer, like picnics or outdoor games.

Another well-known winery in the Barossa Valley is Penfolds, where you can enjoy learning about one of Australia's oldest and most respected wine brands. Many of these wineries also have restaurants that serve locally sourced food, which is perfect for trying regional specialties like barbecued meats and cheese platters. If you're lucky, you might even get a chance to visit during one of the area's famous food and wine festivals, where the best local chefs, wine makers, and artists come together to celebrate everything the Barossa Valley has to offer.

• **Festivals and Events in Adelaide**

Adelaide is often called the "Festival City" because it hosts so many exciting events and festivals throughout the year. Whether you love music, art, or food, you'll find something to enjoy in this vibrant city.

One of the most famous festivals in Adelaide is the **Adelaide Fringe**, held every year in February and March. The festival features hundreds of performances, including comedy shows, theater productions, and live music. It's one of the biggest arts festivals in the world and attracts people from all over the globe. If you're visiting during this time, you'll see the city come to life with colorful performances and fun events.

Another popular event in Adelaide is the **Adelaide Festival of Arts**, which celebrates the city's creative spirit. It's a great place to see amazing performances, exhibitions, and installations from local and international artists. If you love arts and culture, this festival is a must-see.

For food lovers, the **Adelaide Farmers' Market** is a great place to sample local products, like fresh fruit, vegetables, honey, and gourmet snacks. It's held every Sunday and is a fun way to discover the flavors of South Australia.

• **Adelaide's Coastal Spots**

Just a short drive from the city, you'll find some of the best beaches in South Australia. Whether you want to relax in the sun, swim in the clear blue water, or try your hand at surfing, Adelaide's coastline has something for everyone.

One of the most popular beaches in Adelaide is **Glenelg Beach**, a lively spot known for its sandy shore and great swimming conditions. It's a family-friendly beach with plenty of places to eat and things to do. You can take a walk along the **Glenelg Jetty,** rent a bike, or even visit the **Paddle Steamer** to get a taste of what it was like to travel around the area in the past.

Another great beach to visit is **Henley Beach,** known for its relaxed atmosphere and great sunset views. It's a quieter spot where you can enjoy the water and sand, without the crowds. If you love nature, make sure to visit **Encounter Bay,** which is perfect for kayaking, watching dolphins, and spotting wildlife like kangaroos.

If you're more into nature walks, **The Fleurieu Peninsula** is a beautiful area just outside Adelaide, offering great hiking trails, peaceful beaches, and stunning coastal views. The **Deep Creek Conservation Park** is one of the best spots for hiking, with paths that take you through native forests and to breathtaking lookout points.

• Adelaide Hills

For those who love nature, the **Adelaide Hills** are just a short drive from the city and offer a peaceful escape with plenty of outdoor activities. The hills are known for their cool climate, lush forests, and quaint villages. It's a great place to go hiking, picnicking, or simply enjoy the fresh air.

One of the most popular spots in the Adelaide Hills is **Mount Lofty,** where you can hike up to the top and enjoy a stunning view of the city and the surrounding countryside. There's also a botanical garden at the top, where you can relax and enjoy the flowers.

For a more adventurous experience, try **Cleland Wildlife Park.** Here, you can get up close with Australian animals like koalas, kangaroos, and wombats. It's a great way to see some of Australia's most famous wildlife in a natural setting.

• **Adelaide**

Back in the city, Adelaide is full of history, art, and modern attractions. You can explore the **Adelaide Central Market,** which has been around for over 150 years. The market is the perfect place to grab some fresh food or try a delicious local treat. You'll find everything from fresh seafood and cheeses to homemade pastries and organic fruits.

If you're into history, check out **North Terrace,** a street lined with museums, galleries, and historical buildings. The **South Australian Museum** is one of the best places to learn about the history of the region, with exhibits about the area's Aboriginal culture and natural history.

Adelaide also has a thriving music scene. The **Adelaide Entertainment Centre** hosts concerts, shows, and events throughout the year, and the **Lion Arts Centre** is another great venue for performances. If you're a fan of live music or theater, you'll find something exciting to see in the city.

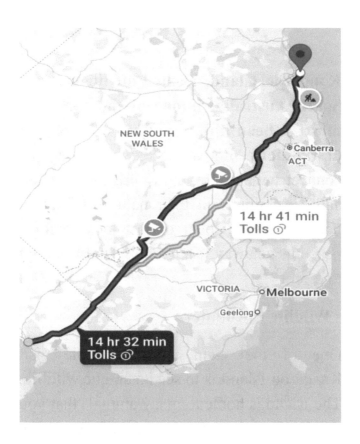

• **The map above shows distance (with time covered) from Sydney central to Adelaide**

Kangaroo Island

Kangaroo Island, located off the coast of South Australia, is one of the country's most beautiful and wildlife-rich destinations. It's a place where you can connect with nature, enjoy pristine beaches, and see animals in their natural habitat. If you're a nature lover or just looking for a peaceful getaway, Kangaroo Island has a lot to offer.

• **Wildlife Encounters**

One of the main reasons people visit Kangaroo Island is to see its unique wildlife. The island is home to many animals that you won't find in other parts of Australia. Kangaroos, of course, are one of the biggest attractions, but there are also koalas, sea lions, echidnas, and many different species of birds. The best part is that these animals live freely in their natural environment, making it a fantastic place for animal lovers.

A popular spot on the island for wildlife watching is **Flinders Chase National Park.** Here, you can see kangaroos hopping across the grassy fields and koalas sleeping in the tall eucalyptus trees. The park is also home to the island's famous **Remarkable Rocks**, a collection of strange and beautiful granite boulders shaped by wind and time. These rocks make for amazing photos, especially when the sunlight changes throughout the day.

Another great place to see wildlife is **Seal Bay Conservation Park**. Here, you can get up close to a large colony of **Australian sea lions**. These playful creatures lounge on the beach, and you can even take a guided tour to learn more about their behavior and habitat. Be sure to keep your distance and respect the sea lions, but it's an unforgettable experience to watch them in their natural home.

• Coastal Scenery and Beaches

Kangaroo Island is famous for its stunning coastal scenery. From towering cliffs to sandy beaches, the island offers breathtaking views at every turn. Whether you're looking to take a relaxing walk, snap some photos, or enjoy a day by the water, the island's coastline won't disappoint.

Vivonne Bay is one of the island's most beautiful beaches. Its clear blue water, white sand, and gentle waves make it a perfect spot for swimming or just relaxing by the shore. It's also a great place for families since the beach is usually quiet and peaceful. If you enjoy fishing, you can try your luck here as well, as the bay is known for its great catch.

For those who like a bit of adventure, **Stokes Bay** is another fantastic spot. To reach the beach, you have to walk through a narrow rock tunnel that opens up to a beautiful, sheltered cove. It's like discovering a hidden beach! The waters here are calm and perfect for swimming or kayaking, and the surrounding cliffs create a dramatic backdrop for photos.

If you're into surfing, you should head to **Pennington Bay**. Known for its great surf breaks, this beach is perfect for surfers of all skill levels. Even if you're not a surfer, it's worth a visit just for the view, as the waves crash against the rocks, creating an amazing sight.

• Hidden Gems and Secluded Beaches

While some parts of Kangaroo Island are popular with tourists, there are also plenty of secluded beaches where you can escape the crowds and enjoy the natural beauty of the island. These hidden gems are perfect for those who want to relax and enjoy some peace and quiet in nature.

One of the most secluded beaches is **Hanson Bay.** This spot is quieter and less visited than other beaches on the island, making it a great place for a peaceful day in nature. The beach is surrounded by thick bushland, and the calm waters are perfect for a swim or a quiet picnic.

Another secret beach to check out is **D'Estrees Bay.** Located on the island's southern coast, this beautiful bay offers wide sandy shores, perfect for long walks or just relaxing in the sun. The beach is also known for its rock pools, where you can explore the tide pools and discover small fish and crabs.

• **Adventure Activities and Outdoor Fun**

Kangaroo Island isn't just for relaxing by the beach—it's also a great place for outdoor activities. Whether you like hiking, kayaking, or cycling, there's something for everyone to enjoy.

If you love hiking, the **Kangaroo Island Wilderness Trail** is a must. This 5-day hike takes you through some of the island's most stunning landscapes, including forests, cliffs, and beaches. You'll pass through Flinders Chase National Park and see amazing wildlife along the way. For those who prefer shorter walks, there are plenty of day trails to choose from, each offering unique views of the island's diverse landscapes.

For an unforgettable adventure, consider kayaking around the coastline. There are several tour companies on the island that offer guided kayaking trips, where you can explore the rugged coastline, see sea lions in the wild, and even paddle through caves and rock formations.

The waters around the island are calm and clear, making it an ideal place to try kayaking for the first time.

Cycling is another popular activity on Kangaroo Island, with several bike-friendly trails winding through the island's countryside. Renting a bike is a great way to see the island's quiet villages, vineyards, and farmland. Along the way, you can stop at local cafés, enjoy a meal, or sample some of the island's delicious produce.

• **Local Food and Culture**

Kangaroo Island is not only about wildlife and natural beauty—it's also a place where you can enjoy some amazing food. The island is known for its fresh, locally sourced ingredients, including seafood, honey, and produce. **Kangaroo Island honey** is a famous treat, and you can visit **Island Beehive** to see how the honey is made and taste some delicious samples. The island's honey has a unique flavor because of the plants the bees pollinate, making it a perfect souvenir to take home.

The island also has a growing wine scene. There are several vineyards on the island where you can sample some local wines and enjoy a meal at a vineyard restaurant. **Dudley Wines** offers stunning views of the island's coastline, while **Kangaroo Island Spirits** is a must-visit for those interested in trying local gin and other spirits.

Another great way to experience the local food is by visiting the **Kangaroo Island Farmers' Market,** which is held on the first Saturday of every month. Here, you can find fresh produce, local cheeses, jams, and baked goods. It's a great place to pick up some souvenirs and support local farmers and producers.

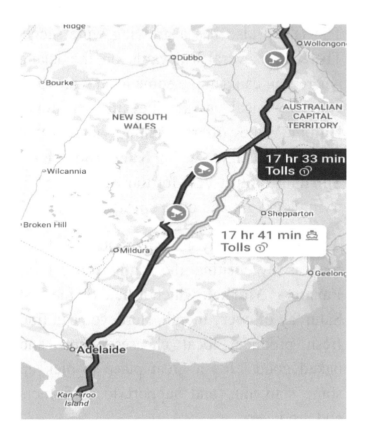

- The map above shows distance (with time covered) from Sydney central to Kangaroo Island

Chapter Seven:

Seven-Day Itinerary for

Australia's Highlights

Day 1: Sydney

On your first day, you'll get to see some of the most famous sights in Sydney, all while soaking in the vibrant atmosphere that makes it so special.

• **Morning**

Start your day with one of the most famous landmarks in the world: the Sydney Opera House. This beautiful building is shaped like sails, and it sits right next to the water in Circular Quay. You can take a guided tour of the Opera House, which will show you the inside of this architectural wonder. You'll get to see the grand concert halls, learn about its history, and maybe even catch a glimpse of a performance if you're lucky.

After visiting the Opera House, take a short walk to the Sydney Harbour Bridge. This bridge is not only a key part of Sydney's skyline but also one of the longest and tallest steel arch bridges in the world. For a truly unforgettable experience, you can go on a BridgeClimb to the top.

The climb takes about 3 hours, but the view from the top is absolutely worth it. You'll be able to see all of Sydney, from the sparkling blue harbour to the city's skyscrapers and the blue mountains in the distance. If you're not up for climbing the bridge, simply enjoy the view from Circular Quay or the Royal Botanic Garden, which is nearby.

• Midday

After your time at the Opera House and Harbour Bridge, head to the Royal Botanic Garden. This particular garden is peaceful.

There, you will have the chance to walk along the shaded paths. You will enjoy the beautiful flowers, and have a picnic while overlooking the harbour. The garden is also home to many birds, so it's fun to look out for colorful parrots and other wildlife.

If you want to take a break and grab some food, head over to Circular Quay. There are plenty of cafes and restaurants where you can enjoy a bite to eat.

Try some classic Australian food like a meat pie or fish and chips, or enjoy a fresh sandwich or salad. Circular Quay is also a great spot to relax and watch the ferries come and go, all while enjoying the stunning views of the harbour.

• Afternoon

In the afternoon, it's time to check out one of Sydney's most famous beaches: Bondi Beach. To get there, you can take a bus or a quick drive from Circular Quay.

Once you arrive, you'll immediately notice why Bondi is so popular. The beach has golden sand, clear blue water, and plenty of surfers catching waves.

If you enjoy swimming or just want to dip your toes in the water, Bondi Beach is the perfect spot. The water is often a bit chilly, but it's refreshing on a hot day.

Even if you're not a swimmer, Bondi Beach is still worth visiting. The Bondi to Coogee coastal walk is one of the best ways to see the area.

This scenic walk stretches for about 6 kilometres and offers beautiful views of the ocean, cliffs, and other smaller beaches like Tamarama and Bronte Beach.

You'll walk past coastal parks, rocky outcrops, and even some amazing rock pools that are perfect for a swim.

It's an easy walk, and along the way, you can stop to take photos, rest, or grab an ice cream.

• Evening

As the evening approaches, head back toward the Darling Harbour area - a vibrant place filled with shops, restaurants and other attractions. You can stroll along the promenade, watch street performers, or enjoy the views of the harbour at sunset. If you're into history and museums, The Australian National Maritime Museum is nearby and worth a visit. Here, you can learn about Australia's rich maritime history and even explore a real submarine.

For an incredible view of the city as it lights up for the night, visit the Sydney Tower Eye. Located in the heart of the city, this tower is the tallest structure in Sydney. Take the elevator up to the observation deck, and you'll have a 360-degree view of the entire city. If you're feeling adventurous, you can also try the Skywalk, which allows you to walk around the outside of the tower with safety gear while enjoying the incredible views.

• **Dinner**

After a fun-filled day, it's time to relax and enjoy some delicious food. Sydney is known for its diverse dining scene, so you'll have plenty of options to choose from. If you're near Darling Harbour, you can find lots of restaurants offering everything from seafood to international dishes. For a classic Australian meal, try a plate of grilled barramundi (a type of fish), or sample some Australian lamb.

If you're near Bondi, there are great spots to eat as well. Many of the cafes and restaurants near the beach have outdoor seating, so you can enjoy your meal while watching the waves roll in. Try a Bondi burger or a fresh salad with locally sourced ingredients. If you love seafood, fish tacos and grilled prawns are also great choices.

Day 2: Blue Mountains

The Blue Mountains are a short drive from Sydney, making them a perfect destination for a day trip. This natural wonder is famous for its stunning views, beautiful landscapes, and unique wildlife. On Day 2 of your Australian adventure, get ready for a day surrounded by nature with towering cliffs, dense forests, and clear waterfalls.

• **Morning**

The Blue Mountains are about 2 hours from Sydney by car, so you can start your day early to make the most of it. You can also take a train from Sydney to Katoomba, the main town in the Blue Mountains. The train ride is a relaxing way to enjoy the countryside as you leave the city behind and head towards the mountains. Once you arrive in Katoomba, you'll be ready to start your adventure.

• Scenic World and the Three Sisters

One of the first stops when you arrive in the Blue Mountains is Scenic World, a popular attraction that gives you amazing views of the area. Scenic World has several fun ways to see the landscape. You can take the Scenic Railway, which is the world's steepest incline railway. It goes down into the valley, and the view as you descend is breathtaking. The railway carriages are designed to lean forward, giving you the feeling that you're flying through the trees. This is a unique way to see the forest up close.

Another must-see at Scenic World is the Scenic Cableway, which takes you up to the top of the mountains. From here, you'll get a wide view of the famous Three Sisters, a group of three tall sandstone peaks. According to local Aboriginal legend, these three rock formations represent three sisters who were turned into stone. The view of the Three Sisters with the surrounding valley is one of the most iconic images of the Blue Mountains.

You can also walk along the Scenic Walkway, which is a boardwalk that winds through the rainforest. This easy walk takes you past towering trees, lush plants, and hidden waterfalls. The cool, damp air and the sounds of birds and water make it a peaceful place to explore. The walk is perfect for families, as it's not too difficult and offers lots of opportunities to take photos.

• **Late Morning**

After visiting Scenic World, head to Echo Point. This is one of the most popular spots to see the Three Sisters from a different angle. Echo Point offers a large viewing platform that overlooks the majestic cliffs and valleys below. The views are absolutely amazing, especially when the sun shines down on the cliffs, creating a blue mist that gives the mountains their name.

From Echo Point, you can also take a short walk to the Glenbrook Lookout. This lookout provides another great spot to view the Blue Mountains, and it's quieter than Echo Point, so it's a good place to relax and enjoy the scenery without too many people around.

• **Afternoon**

The Blue Mountains are known for their amazing nature walks, and in the afternoon, it's time to take one yourself. A popular option is the Prince Henry Cliff Walk, which is a well-maintained path that offers some of the best views of the mountains and valleys. The walk is easy to moderate, and it takes you through beautiful landscapes filled with eucalyptus trees, wildflowers, and scenic lookouts. Along the way, you'll see different views of the Three Sisters, the Jamison Valley, and even some distant waterfalls.

For those who want to see a waterfall up close, the Leura Cascades is another great walk. This beautiful waterfall is located in the village of Leura, just a short drive from Katoomba. The walk to the waterfall is peaceful and offers a chance to spot some local wildlife, such as lyrebirds or kangaroos. The cascading water and the sound of nature all around make this a perfect place to stop for a rest.

• Late Afternoon

After spending the day exploring the mountains and walking through the forests, head back to Katoomba for a relaxing lunch. There are plenty of cafes and restaurants in the town where you can enjoy a meal. If you're looking for something local, try meat pies, a classic Australian dish that's delicious and filling. You can also grab a sandwich or salad if you prefer something lighter.

Another option is to stop by a cafe that offers homemade cakes or scones with jam and cream. Many of the cafes in Katoomba are in historic buildings, so you'll feel like you're stepping back in time as you enjoy your meal. Take your time, relax, and enjoy the charming atmosphere of this mountain town.

• **Evening**

As the day winds down, it's time to head back to Sydney. If you're driving, you can take a scenic route back and stop at different lookouts along the way for more views of the mountains. If you're taking the train, enjoy the ride back as you reflect on the beauty of the Blue Mountains.

You might want to stop at Wentworth Falls on your way back. These waterfalls are located about 20 minutes from Katoomba and are another stunning spot to see. The falls are tall and dramatic, with water plunging down into the valley below. There are also great walking tracks around the falls, so you can enjoy another short nature walk if you have time before heading back to the city.

Day 3: Cairns and Great Barrier Reef

On Day 3, get ready for an unforgettable adventure in Cairns, the gateway to the Great Barrier Reef. Cairns is known for its stunning coral reefs, crystal-clear waters, and lush rainforests. This day is packed with exciting activities, from exploring the world-famous Great Barrier Reef to taking a peaceful walk through the ancient rainforests nearby. Whether you're snorkeling, diving, or just soaking up the natural beauty, Cairns has something for everyone.

• **Morning**

Start your day early, as you'll want to make the most of your time on the Great Barrier Reef. Most tours leave from Cairns, and you can choose between a variety of boats that take you to different reef locations. Reef boats typically set sail in the morning, so make sure you've had a good breakfast and are ready for an action-packed day.

The Great Barrier Reef is home to an amazing variety of sea life, including colorful fish, turtles, and even dolphins and sharks. The reef is one of the most popular natural attractions in the world, and it's easy to see why.

As the boat heads toward the reef, you'll notice the water turning from a deep blue to a lighter turquoise color. This is the shallow part of the reef, where the coral is most colorful and teeming with life. Most tours will take you to areas where you can easily swim and snorkel right off the boat.

• **Snorkeling or Diving on the Great Barrier Reef**

Once you arrive at the reef, it's time to get into the water! If you've never snorkeled before, don't worry—many reef tours offer instructions and equipment, so you can get the hang of it quickly. You'll wear a mask and snorkel, which allows you to breathe while you float on the surface of the water, and fins to help you swim easily.

As you look down into the clear blue water, you'll see coral gardens filled with fish in all colors of the rainbow. You might even spot a green sea turtle gliding by or a stingray swimming over the sand. The reef is like a giant underwater city, full of life and beauty. You might also see schools of clownfish, parrotfish, or butterflyfish darting through the coral.

For those who are more experienced or want to try something new, many reef tours also offer scuba diving options. If you're already a certified diver, you can join a guided dive to explore the reef's deeper areas, where you might encounter larger sea creatures like reef sharks or giant groupers. If you've never dived before, you can take a short course called introductory diving, where you'll get a brief lesson on how to use the diving equipment.

Whether you're snorkeling or diving, being in the water and seeing the Great Barrier Reef up close is truly a once-in-a-lifetime experience.

• **Lunch on the Reef**

After a morning of snorkeling or diving, most tours will offer lunch onboard the boat. Enjoy a relaxing meal with views of the reef. Lunch often includes light and refreshing options, such as sandwiches, salads, and tropical fruits like pineapple and watermelon. This is a great time to chat with fellow travelers about your experiences in the water and take in the beautiful surroundings.

If you're lucky, you might spot more marine life as you eat, like dolphins jumping out of the water in the distance or a sea eagle flying overhead.

• **Afternoon**

After spending the morning on the reef, it's time to head back to shore. But the adventure isn't over yet! In the afternoon, you'll visit the Daintree Rainforest, one of the oldest rainforests in the world. It's home to a wide range of unique plants and animals. This lush, green rainforest is full of surprises, and there's plenty to see and do.

A great way to start is by taking a guided walk through the rainforest. A knowledgeable guide will lead you through the forest, pointing out interesting plants like kapok trees and explaining the history of the area. You might also see cassowaries, large flightless birds with striking blue and black feathers, or tree frogs hiding in the leaves.

Many tours also include a boat ride on the Daintree River. The river is home to a number of wildlife species, including crocodiles, kingfishers, and bats. Keep your eyes peeled as you float down the river for a chance to spot these fascinating creatures in their natural habitat.

If you have more time, consider visiting the Daintree Discovery Centre, where you can learn even more about the plants and animals that live in the rainforest. The center has an aerial walkway that gives you a bird's-eye view of the trees and a canopy tower for even higher views. This is a great spot for photos and to see how big and lush the rainforest really is.

• Late Afternoon

After a day full of adventure, it's time to head back to Cairns. The drive from the Daintree Rainforest to Cairns is about 1.5 hours, so you'll have time to relax and reflect on the incredible experiences of the day. The road takes you through beautiful landscapes, with the rainforest on one side and the Coral Sea on the other.

Once you arrive back in Cairns, you'll have some free time to unwind. If you're feeling hungry, you can grab a bite to eat at one of the many restaurants along the Cairns Esplanade, which offers beautiful views of the ocean. Cairns is known for its tropical fruits, seafood, and other local dishes, so you might want to try something new, like barramundi (a type of fish) or a tropical fruit salad.

Day 4: Whitsunday Islands

On Day 4 of your Australian adventure, get ready to experience some of the most beautiful beaches and islands in the world. Your day will take you to the Whitsunday Islands, a group of 74 islands located in the heart of the Great Barrier Reef. This is one of the most famous and stunning areas of Australia, known for its sparkling blue waters, white sandy beaches, and incredible coral reefs. Today's adventure will include a sailing tour around Whitehaven Beach, one of the most famous beaches in the world, along with stops at other nearby islands for swimming, snorkeling, and relaxing.

• **Morning**

Start your day early as you board a comfortable sailing boat for an exciting journey to Whitehaven Beach. Located on Whitsunday Island, Whitehaven Beach is famous for its soft, white sand that's made up of 98% pure silica. This makes the sand incredibly soft and bright, almost like powdered sugar. It stretches over 7 kilometers along the coast, offering plenty of space to walk, relax, and enjoy the beauty of the surroundings.

The sailing tour will take you through Whitsunday Passage, a beautiful stretch of water between the islands. You'll cruise past smaller islands and rocky outcrops, with the wind gently guiding the boat. Along the way, you might see dolphins swimming in the water or even a whale if you're visiting during the right season (usually from June to November).

As you approach Whitehaven Beach, you'll notice the clear turquoise water and the fine, white sand. The boat will anchor near the shore, and you'll have plenty of time to hop off and explore. If you like, you can take a walk along the beach, enjoying the peaceful atmosphere and stunning views. The sand is so fine that it feels like you're walking on soft powder, and the water is warm and inviting.

• **Mid-Morning**

Once you step onto Whitehaven Beach, you'll immediately feel like you've arrived in paradise. The sand is so soft, and the water so clear, it's easy to see why this beach is regularly listed among the top beaches in the world. You can swim in the shallow waters, float on the gentle waves, or just relax on the beach and soak up the sun.

One of the most popular spots on Whitehaven Beach is Hill Inlet, a picturesque area where the tides create swirling patterns in the sand, forming beautiful, ever-changing shapes. You can walk up to the Hill Inlet Lookout for a panoramic view of the inlet, the white sand, and the bright blue waters. It's one of the most photographed spots in Australia, and you'll want to take a few pictures to remember the moment.

During your time at Whitehaven Beach, you can also enjoy a picnic lunch onboard the sailing boat. Many tours offer sandwiches, fresh fruit, and drinks, so you can relax while taking in the views. You might even be lucky enough to spot some sea turtles or small fish swimming just below the surface.

• **Afternoon**

After spending time on Whitehaven Beach, your sailing tour will take you to some of the nearby islands for more adventure. Snorkeling is one of the highlights of visiting the Whitsundays, as the waters are full of marine life, including colorful coral, fish, and even giant clams. The reefs around the Whitsundays are part of the Great Barrier Reef, so the underwater world is teeming with life.

Most tours will stop at a location where you can put on your snorkeling gear and jump into the warm, clear water. You might see schools of fish darting between the corals, butterfly fish, and parrotfish swimming around the rocks. If you're lucky, you could also spot a giant sea turtle or a ray gliding gracefully through the water.

If you're not into snorkeling, you can also enjoy the boat's facilities or go for a walk around one of the nearby islands. Many of the Whitsunday Islands are small and uninhabited, which means they're peaceful and perfect for a relaxing walk in the sun. You might find that the only sounds you hear are the rustling of the trees and the gentle lapping of the water on the shore.

• Late Afternoon

As the day begins to wind down, your sailing tour will head back to Airlie Beach, the main hub for visitors to the Whitsunday

Islands. Along the way, you can relax on the boat and enjoy the last views of the islands. The water will be a little calmer in the afternoon, and you might even see a rainbow lorikeet flying by or a pelican gliding over the waves.

Once back in Airlie Bcach, you'll have some free time to explore the town. Airlie Beach is a laid-back, tropical town with plenty of cafes, shops, and restaurants. It's a great place to grab a bite to eat after your day on the water. You could try a local seafood dish, such as barramundi or prawns, or enjoy a refreshing tropical drink.

Airlie Beach is also home to a lagoon pool right by the waterfront. If you have time and want to cool off, you can take a dip in the lagoon, which is safe for swimming and offers great views of the ocean.

Day 5: Uluru

Day 5 of your Australian adventure takes you to one of the country's most iconic landmarks: Uluru.

Also known as Ayers Rock, Uluru is a giant sandstone monolith. It is a sacred site for the Anangu people, the traditional owners of the land, and it has been part of their culture for thousands of years.

Today, you will get to experience the magic of Uluru during sunrise or sunset, learn about the area's deep cultural history, and end your day with a stunning view of the stars.

• Morning

Start your day early by catching the famous sunrise at Uluru. The sight of the sun rising over this massive rock is truly breathtaking.

As the sun climbs higher in the sky, it slowly changes the color of Uluru from a deep red to bright oranges and yellows, and finally to soft pinks.

The changing colors of the rock, especially at sunrise, are one of the most famous natural wonders in the world.

You will likely visit one of the designated viewing areas, like Talinguru Nyakunytjaku, which offers a great spot to watch the sunrise.

Here, you'll have a clear view of Uluru and Kata Tjuta (another nearby rock formation), and you can take some time to admire the view, snap a few photos, and simply enjoy the peaceful moment.

Uluru is around 348 meters high and over 9 kilometers in circumference, so it's a massive rock! As the sun rises and the light shifts, you can really see the different textures and layers of the rock.

Some people also like to take a guided walk around the base of Uluru to learn more about its cultural significance, but today is all about soaking in the beauty of the sunrise.

• **Late Morning**

After watching the sunrise, it's time to learn about the deep cultural history of Uluru and the Anangu people, the traditional owners of the land. You can visit the Uluru-Kata Tjuta Cultural Centre, where you can learn about the rock's significance, the Anangu culture, and the importance of the surrounding landscape.

The Anangu people have lived in the area around Uluru for thousands of years, and their connection to the land is central to their way of life. At the cultural center, you'll find exhibits that explain the traditional stories and beliefs of the Anangu people, including their Tjukurpa (Dreamtime) stories, which explain how the world came to be. There are also displays on the region's plants, animals, and history, so you can gain a deeper understanding of how the Anangu people have lived and thrived in the harsh Outback environment for centuries.

You can also join a guided walk with an Anangu guide, who will share stories about the land and explain the significance of various features of Uluru and its surroundings.

Some of these walks include visiting sacred sites around the base of the rock, where you'll hear about traditional practices, food sources, and how the Anangu people have passed down their knowledge for generations.

For lunch, you can enjoy a picnic in the area or dine at one of the local restaurants, where you can try some native Australian foods like kangaroo, camel, or even bush tomatoes. Many local chefs use these ingredients to create modern dishes that celebrate the unique flavors of the Outback.

• **Afternoon**

In the afternoon, it's time to head over to Kata Tjuta, another important rock formation near Uluru. Kata Tjuta, which means "many heads" in the local language, is made up of 36 large domes of rock and is just as impressive as Uluru. The site is sacred to the Anangu people and is home to many important Dreamtime stories.

One of the best ways to experience Kata Tjuta is by doing the Valley of the Winds walk, which takes you through the rugged terrain between the domes.

This walk is a bit challenging but very rewarding, with amazing views of the rock formations and the surrounding desert. Along the way, you'll pass through shady groves and rocky valleys, and you may even see some of the local wildlife, such as wallabies and perentie lizards.

If you prefer a less strenuous walk, there is also a shorter trail to Walpa Gorge, which is an easy walk and offers a fantastic view of the domes of Kata Tjuta. This is a great option if you want to take in the beauty of the area without the longer hike.

• **Evening**

As the day winds down, it's time for the iconic sunset at Uluru. Just like the sunrise, the sunset at Uluru is a magical experience. The rock changes colors again as the sun sets, and it's a truly unforgettable sight. Many visitors choose to watch the sunset from Talinguru Nyakunytjaku or Sunset Viewing Area, where you can see Uluru glow as the sun dips below the horizon.

At sunset, the colors of Uluru shift from reds and oranges to darker shades of purple and blue. It's a moment of stillness, and many people choose to sit quietly and watch the light show unfold in front of them.

• **Night**

After sunset, the sky over Uluru becomes a stargazer's paradise. The Outback is far from city lights, making it one of the best places in Australia to see the stars. The night sky is incredibly clear, and the stars seem to stretch on forever. You can either relax and gaze at the stars on your own, or you can join a stargazing tour.

These tours are led by expert guides who will point out the constellations and tell you stories about the night sky. You'll see famous constellations like the Southern Cross and Orion, and you may even spot a few planets if the timing is right. If you're lucky, you might also see a shooting star streak across the sky.

The vast desert sky is perfect for stargazing, and the peace and quiet of the Outback make it a great way to end your day. It's a magical moment to reflect on the beauty of the day and the ancient culture of the land.

Day 6: Melbourne

On Day 6 of your Australian adventure, it's time to head to Melbourne, the vibrant cultural heart of Australia. Melbourne is a city known for its thriving art scene, unique cafes, and hidden laneways filled with street art and quirky shops. Whether you're an art lover, a foodie, or someone who loves exploring the unexpected, Melbourne has something special for you.

• Morning

Melbourne is famous for its coffee culture, so your day should begin with a stop at one of its many cafes. Whether you're after a creamy cappuccino, a strong espresso, or a perfectly brewed flat white, you're in the right place.

One of the most popular areas to start your morning is in Degraves Street, a small laneway filled with cafes where you can watch the world go by while enjoying a freshly brewed coffee. The laneways of Melbourne are not just about coffee, though—they are home to some of the best street art in the world.

As you sip your coffee, take a moment to look around. The laneways are packed with colorful murals, graffiti, and posters that make the streets feel like an open-air gallery.

Hosier Lane is one of the most famous laneways for street art, with its ever-changing wall of colors and designs. Artists from all over the world leave their mark here, making it a great spot to take photos.

The laneways themselves are full of surprises. You'll find hidden boutiques, restaurants, and art galleries tucked away behind narrow alleyways. A walk through these streets feels like uncovering little secrets in the city.

Don't forget to stop and admire the floral installations and artistic windows that make Melbourne's streets feel alive.

• Late Morning

After you've soaked in the atmosphere of the laneways, it's time to dive into Melbourne's art scene. The city is home to some incredible galleries and museums, and a visit to any of them will help you understand why Melbourne is considered one of the most creative cities in Australia.

The National Gallery of Victoria (NGV) is a must-see. It's Australia's oldest and most visited public art museum, and it's home to an impressive collection of art from around the world. The gallery's International Art collection includes pieces from European masters, Asian art, and Indigenous

Australian art. Don't forget to visit the beautiful NGV Garden, which features stunning sculptures and water features.

If modern art interests you, make sure to stop by the Australian Centre for Contemporary Art (ACCA). This gallery showcases the works of both local and international contemporary artists and is known for its thought-provoking exhibitions. Melbourne's art scene also includes street art and installations, which you can discover on your walk through the laneways.

• **Lunch**

By now, you're likely starting to feel hungry after all the walking, so it's time to enjoy lunch at one of Melbourne's famous food spots. Melbourne is home to a diverse range of cuisines, thanks to its multicultural population. Whether you're craving Italian pizza, Asian street food, or something a little more unusual, you'll find it here.

One popular area for lunch is Chinatown, which is home to some of Melbourne's best dumplings, noodles, and dim sum. If you prefer something more modern, head to Fitzroy, a neighborhood known for its trendy cafes and restaurants. Here you can enjoy everything from vegan burgers to craft beers. Melbourne also has a growing brunch culture, so don't miss the chance to try some of the city's famous avocado toast or eggs benedict at one of its many brunch spots.

• **Afternoon**

After lunch, it's time to take a relaxing break in Melbourne's Royal Botanic Gardens. This peaceful park in the center of the city is a great place to relax after a busy morning. You can walk around the beautifully landscaped gardens, spot local wildlife like koalas and kookaburras, or simply find a quiet spot to sit and enjoy the view.

If you're in the mood for more culture, head over to Federation Square. This cultural precinct is home to several of Melbourne's key museums, including the Australian Centre for the Moving Image (ACMI) and the Ian Potter Centre. You can catch an interactive film exhibit, learn about Australian history, or simply explore the unique architecture of the square itself.

Federation Square is also home to a variety of cafes, shops, and galleries, making it a great spot to spend some time.

• **Evening**

As the day winds down, Melbourne's nightlife and dining scene come alive.

Whether you're looking for a quiet spot to relax or a lively venue to enjoy a drink, Melbourne has something for every mood. If you love craft beers, head to Collingwood or Fitzroy, where you'll find local breweries and bars offering a wide range of brews.

For a more upscale experience, you might want to check out the Eau De Vie, a cocktail bar known for its creative drinks.

Melbourne is also a great place for dinner. Whether you want to try some modern Australian cuisine at a fine-dining restaurant or indulge in a relaxed meal at a buzzy pub, there are plenty of options.

For something really special, try Attica, one of the top restaurants in the city, known for its innovative dishes using native Australian ingredients.

Day 7: Great Ocean Road

On the final day of your Australian adventure, you'll be treated to one of the most beautiful road trips in the world.

The Great Ocean Road, which stretches along the southern coast of Australia, is a must-see for anyone visiting the country.

This scenic drive takes you along stunning coastlines, past famous beaches, and through lush forests.

With plenty of amazing stops along the way, it's the perfect way to wrap up your seven-day trip.

• Morning

Start your day early in the morning, as the Great Ocean Road is a long route with lots to see and do.

If you're staying in Melbourne, it takes about 1.5 to 2 hours to reach the start of the road, where you'll begin your adventure.

As you start the drive, you'll immediately be taken by the beautiful ocean views, the sound of the waves crashing on the shore, and the refreshing sea breeze.

The road itself runs from Torquay to Allansford, and along the way, you'll pass through several charming seaside towns, each with its own unique attractions.

As you drive, keep your camera ready—every corner brings new breathtaking sights.

• **First Stop**

Your first stop should be Bells Beach, one of Australia's most famous surf spots. Known for its incredible waves, Bells Beach has been the setting for world-renowned surfing competitions.

Even if you're not into surfing, it's a great place to watch surfers ride massive waves or simply enjoy the beauty of the beach.

If you're interested in learning more about surf culture, make sure to check out the nearby Surf World Museum in Torquay, which showcases the history of surfing in Australia.

You can learn about the evolution of surfboards and the stories behind some of the greatest surfers in the world.

• The Twelve Apostles

Next, drive along the coast until you reach one of the most famous spots on the Great Ocean Road: the Twelve Apostles.

These incredible limestone formations rise majestically from the ocean, creating a dramatic and unforgettable scene. Although there were originally twelve of these rocky spires, only eight remain, but they still make for an amazing view.

You'll find a large viewing platform at the Twelve Apostles, which gives you a perfect spot to take photos. The sight of these towering rocks against the backdrop of the crashing waves is something you'll never forget. If you're lucky, you might even see a rainbow or some wild seabirds flying around.

While you're at the Twelve Apostles, consider taking a helicopter ride. From the air, you'll get an even better perspective of the rock formations and the surrounding coast, making it a once-in-a-lifetime experience.

• Loch Ard Gorge

Just a short drive from the Twelve Apostles, you'll find Loch Ard Gorge, a hidden gem that offers both natural beauty and historical significance. This beach is named after the shipwreck of the Loch Ard in 1878. Only two people survived the wreck, and their story is told through informative signs and displays at the site.

Take a walk down to the beach and feel the sand between your toes while looking up at the towering cliffs around you. You can also explore the various walking trails that take you around the gorge, giving you different viewpoints of the area.

• **Otway National Park**

After the Twelve Apostles and Loch Ard Gorge, continue your journey inland through Otway National Park.

This beautiful park is known for its lush rainforests, towering trees, and picturesque waterfalls.

Take a short detour to visit Hopetoun Falls or Triplet Falls, both located in the heart of the park. These waterfalls are stunning, and you can get up close to them by following the walking trails.If you enjoy nature walks, the Otway Fly Tree Top Walk is another great option. This elevated walkway takes you high above the forest floor, where you can see the trees from a new perspective.

The views of the rainforest are especially magical after a light rain, when the air feels fresh and the forest seems alive with sound.

• Lunch Stop

By now, you might be ready to stop for lunch. The towns of Lorne and Apollo Bay are perfect places to take a break. Both towns are right on the coast and offer a variety of lunch options. If you're in the mood for fresh seafood, you can try local fish and chips, or enjoy a light meal at a café by the beach. After lunch, take some time to relax and soak up the beautiful surroundings.

In Apollo Bay, you might also want to visit the Great Ocean Road Visitor Centre for more information on the area. They offer helpful tips on what to see, and you can pick up some souvenirs to remember your trip.

• Afternoon

As the day continues, head toward the Bay of Islands, another stunning spot on the Great Ocean Road. This area is less crowded than some of the other spots, but just as beautiful. The Bay of Islands is made up of several small islands and rock formations scattered just off the coast. You can stop at the viewing platform to take in the scenery or, if you're feeling adventurous, walk down to the beach and explore the area.

The clear blue water and the quiet, unspoiled landscape make this a peaceful and relaxing place to end your day's journey.

• Evening

After a full day of stunning sights, it's time to head back to Melbourne. The drive back takes about 3 hours, so you'll likely arrive in the evening. Reflect on the beautiful places you've seen, from the powerful waves at Bells Beach to the towering Twelve

Apostles, and all the amazing beaches and rainforests in between.

OTHER BOOKS RECOMMENDATION

Dear Reader,

If you liked this guide, **Ethan** suggests checking out for his other books you might want to add to your reading list.

Thank you for being a valued reader! He looks forward to accompanying you on many more literary journeys.

A KIND GESTURE

Dear Fellow Travelers,

Your feedback on the guide is important to **Ethan**. If it made your **trip** more magical, he'd appreciate it if you left a review and shared your experience with others. By spreading the word, you'll help fellow travelers have amazing adventures too.

Thank you for being part of this community of great adventurers. Your kind gesture in leaving a review and recommending the guide is a meaningful contribution to the shared joy of exploration.

Safe travels and happy exploring!
Ethan J. McNally

TRAVEL NOTE

TRAVEL NOTE

TRAVEL NOTE

TRAVEL NOTE

TRAVEL NOTE

_____

_____

_____

_____

_____

_____

_____

_____

_____

_____

_____

TRAVEL NOTE

_____

_____

_____

_____

_____

_____

_____

_____

_____

_____

_____

TRAVEL NOTE

_____

_____

_____

_____

_____

_____

_____

_____

_____

_____

TRAVEL NOTE

TRAVEL NOTE

TRAVEL NOTE